Snow Business

A Study of the International Ski Industry

Simon Hudson

CASSELL

Cassell

Wellington House	370 Lexington Avenue
125 Strand	New York
London WC2R 0BB	NY 10017–6550

www.cassell.co.uk

First published 2000

British Library Cataloguing-in-Publication Data

A catalogue record for this book is available from the British Library.

ISBN   0 304 70470 9 (hb)

  0 304 70471 7 (pb)

Designed and typeset by Ben Cracknell Studios

Printed and bound in Great Britain
by Cromwell Press Ltd, Trowbridge, Wiltshire

Contents

CONTENTS

Acknowledgements

I would like to thank all the people in the ski industry who helped me in compiling the material for this book. I am especially indebted to Colin Mathews from Meriski, Debbie Marshal from Crystal Holidays and Caroline Stuart-Taylor from the Ski Club of Great Britain.

I am also extremely grateful to Tim Nightingale, Steve Pickles and the Tourist Office in Verbier for providing me with some excellent photographic material for the book.

Introduction

It is estimated that over 65 million skiers exist worldwide. About 43 per cent of that market is located in Europe, 34 per cent in the Americas and 20 per cent in Asia. The industry's growth rate over the last decade has been remarkable: the globalization of skiing is quite apparent with the influx of foreign visitors to international destinations increasing dramatically every year. Today, skiing means big business for those involved in the operation of resorts – whether running hotels or rental apartments/chalets, restaurants, ski-lifts, or clothing and equipment shops. Manufacturers of ski equipment and clothing form another major business, and tour operators and transport companies all derive substantial proportions of their business from skiing.

How much the ski industry is worth worldwide is difficult to gauge. The UK ski industry alone is worth approximately £200 million to operators, and directly employs over 3000 individuals. Sales of ski goods, selling from over 700 outlets, were valued at £54.1 million last year. Statistics from the USA indicate in excess of $3 billion in annual revenues for American resorts, split between sales of lift tickets and ski shops. But despite its importance to the tourism industry, skiing has been poorly served by academic texts. For the industry practitioner, the research student, or even the skier, finding information on this dynamic and unique industry is a hard task. Books and articles are mostly dedicated to to the art of skiing, and very seldom to the industry dynamics. This book encapsulates those very dynamics that make the industry such an exciting and intriguing area of study.

Technically speaking, it is no longer just the ski industry or ski business – rather the ski and snowboard industry – but in this book, 'ski' and 'skier' are used as convenient umbrella nouns. The first chapter begins by looking at tourism overall, and the place of the skiing market within the industry. This is followed by an analysis of the evolution of winter sports, plotting the growth from early winter holidays taken in the late nineteenth century to modern-day, mass-packaged skiing holidays. A case study on the Ski Club of Great Britain illustrates the influence the British have had on the evolution of winter sports.

Chapter 2 provides statistics on the market for winter sports holidays worldwide. Although the USA and Japan account for a high percentage of skiers, there are many options available to skiers in terms of destinations. A profile of these destinations is given, and a case study on the history of Verbier in Switzerland provides an example of the growth of a European resort.

The channels of distribution used to attract customers to the slopes are a critical element in the study of the ski industry. Increasingly, changes in both the structure of the industry and in technology have required organizations to reassess their distribution strategies. Chapter 3 takes a closer look at the strategies employed on both sides of the Atlantic. Destinations in North America have traditionally sought to market their products and services directly to skiers, whereas destinations in Europe rely on tour operators to bring British skiers to the slopes. This chapter focuses on the operations of such tour operators, using Crystal Holidays as a case study.

Chapter 4 reviews the academic literature related to skiing and consumer behaviour. The first section is an overview of general research into the skiing industry, including participation rates, and demographics of existing skiers together with their consumption patterns.The second part of the chapter contains a more detailed analysis of studies concerning the motivations of skiers. The case study is an example of an English company, Meriski, that has been successful in targeting and satisfying one segment of the skiing market.

Chapter 5 focuses on the location and development of ski resorts, and the management and marketing of these resorts on both sides of the Atlantic. The physical conditions necessary for a successful ski destination are examined, and two scenarios for the development of tourism in Alpine areas are discussed. The professionalism of resort owners in North America is compared to the more unpredictable and fragmented efforts of European resorts, highlighted by the case study on the marketing of Whistler in Canada.

For a growing number of skiers, the sport represents one of the great dilemmas and conflicts between recreational enjoyment of the countryside and the conservation of the fragile Alpine and mountain areas where skiing inevitably takes place. Chapter 6 looks at the impact of skiing on the environment and at the emerging concept of sustainability. The author then provides a model for the greening of ski resorts that shows the relationships between the key interest groups – tourists, operators, conservation groups, marketers, developers, management, and legislators – and their varying influences on the resort's environmental policies. The model is operationalized using Verbier in Switzerland as a case study.

The final chapter looks at the future prospects for the ski industry, based on forecasts, trends and attitudes to winter sports. Technology is likely to have a huge impact on the skiing product and how it is distributed. This is discussed, along with recommendations for those marketing the skiing product and the destinations that provide winter sports. The author argues for deeper segmentation of both the existing and potential market, and makes some predictions for the future of the ski industry – a future which, though uncertain, offers some exciting prospects.

Abbreviations

ABTA   Association of British Travel Agents (UK)
AITO   Association of Independent Tour Operators
BPE   Barclays Private Equity
BSF   British Ski and Snowboard Federation
CTC   Canadian Tourism Commission
FIS   Fédération Internationale de Ski
MINOS Mountain International Opinion Survey
MMC   Monopolies and Mergers Commission (UK)
NSAA National Ski Areas Association (US)
SAP   Société d'Aménagement de la Plagne
SCGB Ski Club of Great Britain
SIA   Ski Industry Association
WRA   Whistler Resort Association
WTO   World Tourism Organization
WTTC World Travel and Tourism Council

CHAPTER 1

Tourism and Snow Business

INTRODUCTION

This chapter begins by looking at the position of the skiing market within the broader discipline of sports tourism. The next part of the chapter analyses the evolution of winter sports and is followed by sections on alternative winter sports that exist today, and on artificial ski slopes. The chapter concludes with a case study on the Ski Club of Great Britain.

1.1 THE GROWTH OF SPORTS TOURISM

The significance of tourism

Over the past few decades, tourism has emerged as one of the world's major industries, exceeding the importance of many manufacturing industries and other services in terms of sales, employment and foreign currency earnings. The growth of the tourism industry has occurred in both industrialized and developing countries, and while evidence indicating the sheer size of tourism is well known and extensively written about elsewhere (Burkart and Medlik 1989; Cooper 1989; Edgell 1990), straightforward statistics demonstrating its scale are worth reiterating. According to World Tourism Organization analyses (WTO 1992), international tourism receipts grew faster than world trade in goods and services in the 1980s (9.6 per cent between 1980 and 1990). Tourism is now ranked third (after petroleum and motor products) in the list of global export categories, and the WTO expects this growth to continue.

The World Travel and Tourism Council (WTTC 1995), an industry-sponsored, pro-tourism pressure group, claims that tourism is the world's largest industry; is the world's largest employer and creator of jobs; accounts for one in nine global jobs; represents 11 per cent of global wages; is responsible for 11 per cent of world GDP; and accounts for 11 per cent of non-food consumer retailing. The WTTC suggests that in 1995, travel and tourism generated US$3.4 trillion in gross output, and provided direct and indirect employment for 212 million people. By the year 2005, it estimates that travel and tourism will double in size (112.3 per cent in nominal terms), and increase output by 54.6 per cent in real terms. The WTO (1998) states that receipts from international tourism have increased by an average of 9 per cent annually for the past sixteen years to reach US$423 billion in 1996. During the same period, international arrivals rose by a yearly average of 4.6 per cent to reach 594 million in 1996. The WTO forecasts that international arrivals will top 700 million by the year 2000 and one billion by 2010. Likewise, earnings are predicted to grow to US$621 billion by the year 2000 and US$1550 billion by 2010.

These figures emphasize the sheer scale of tourism, the huge range of economic, social and political actions that can affect it, and the impact that it can have on the external socio-political environment. It is only recently that tourism has been considered worthy of serious business endeavour or academic study. However, the figures above support the notion that the tourism industry is of sufficient economic importance, and its impacts upon economies, environments and societies are large enough, for the subject of tourism to deserve serious consideration.

Tourism as an academic activity

The case for the study of tourism as a distinct academic activity has been made (notably through *Annals of Tourism Research*). However, while tourism rightly constitutes a domain of study, it currently lacks the level of theoretical underpinning which would allow it to become a discipline (Cooper, Fletcher, Gilbert and Wanhill 1993). The popularity of tourism as a subject, and the recognition of its importance by governments, has accelerated its study, and tourism now has its own small, but growing, academic community. Many text books provide descriptions of the tourism industry, for example, Burkart and Medlik (1989), Cleverdon and Edwards (1982), Hodgson (1987), Holloway (1990), Lundberg (1989) and McIntosh and Goeldner (1986). Others texts are of a more applied nature, examining the management or marketing of tourism (see Holloway and Plant 1988; Middleton 1988; Witt and Moutinho 1994). Books studying the development of tourism have been written by Pearce (1987, 1995), Smith (1983) and Robinson (1976); there are also books concentrating on the *effects* of this development. Mathieson and Wall's (1982) broad review of the economic, social and physical impacts of tourism is still widely cited, but lately others have focused on the contemporary impacts in a more critical manner (Burns and Holden 1995; Krippendorf 1987).

The content and range of tourism books generally reflect those of the wider journal literature. Descriptions of the structure, operation and management of the industry, and of its attempts to influence consumer demand via marketing strategies, can be found in such journals as *Tourism Management, International Tourism Management, Travel and Tourism Analyst,* and the *Service Industries Journal*. Sinclair and Stabler (1993) suggest, however, that there is little research on the tourism industry and its operation which is analytical in emphasis, providing explanations of the processes that occur, and their causes and effects. They believe that the interrelationships between the industry, the consumer and the destination have been neglected, largely because modelling has been insufficiently integrated.

Journal literature on the spatial development and interrelationships characterizing the tourism industry is well represented in *Journal of Travel Research, Journal of Leisure Research,* and *Tourist Review,* and contributions have also been included in specialist geographic journals such as *Geography* and *GeoJournal*. Examination of the effects of the tourism industry and tourism development is varied. Journals such as *Annals of Tourism Research, Leisure Studies,* and *Tourism Management* have consistently carried articles of this nature. More recently, there has also been a growing awareness of the broad range of impacts that tourism businesses may have on culture and the environment, reflected in new academic journals such as the *Journal of Sustainable Tourism*.

Definitions

Samuel Pegg reported the use of 'tour-ist' as a new word for travellers in the eighteenth century; England's *Sporting Magazine* introduced the word 'tourism' in 1811. Yet despite the fact that the word has now been part of the English language for nearly two centuries, there is still no universally accepted operational definition for tourism. Tourism is a multidimensional, multifaceted activity, that touches many lives and many different economic activities. Not surprisingly, tourism has therefore proved difficult to define. However, as tourism has become more important economically, the terminology used to describe it is becoming increasingly precise (Hunt and Layne 1992). Some analysts (Cooper *et al.* 1993) have adopted the definition by Mathieson and Wall (1982, p. 1) who described tourism as 'the temporary movement of people to destinations outside their normal place of work and residence, the activities taken during their stay in those destinations and the facilities created to cater for their needs'. A similar definition by Burkart and Medlik (1989) also identifies the inclusion of those activities (like skiing) which are involved in the stay or visit to the destination. Others prefer a more holistic definition that acknowledges the consequential aspect (i.e. the 'cost' in human and environmental terms) of the relationship between supply and demand. Burns and Holden (1995) for example, embrace the words of Jafari Jafari (1977, p. 8) who defined tourism as 'a study of man away from his usual habitat, of the industry which responds to his needs, and the impacts that both he and the industry have on the host socio-cultural, economic, and physical environment'.

Gilbert (1990) believes that since current definitions of tourism have been determined for economists, they are not adequate for marketers. He suggests that the simplistic view of tourist behaviour could be rejected and replaced with a new understanding of the tourist as a consumer who demonstrates particular actions or behaviour. These actions involve the needs, motivation, attitudes, values, personality and perceptions that all lead to specific preferences for tourism-related activities. To carry this argument further, the study of tourist consumer behaviour should not only seek to understand the choice process of tourists, but should endeavour to comprehend the range of constraints preventing non-tourists from becoming tourists. Gilbert proposes a definition promulgating a social under-standing of tourism, and describes tourism as 'one part of recreation which involves travel to a less familiar destination or community, for a short-term period, in order to satisfy a consumer need for one or a combination of activities' (p. 25).

In addition, the definitions provided above do not clarify what is included in the classification of tourism demand and supply measurement. An extended classifica-tion system of tourism demand delineating the main purpose of visits by major groups was developed based upon that first proposed by the United Nations (United States Bureau of the Census 1979). The major groups (shown in Figure 1.1) include:

1. Leisure, recreation and holidays;
2. Visiting friends and relatives;
3. Business and professional;
4. Health treatment;
5. Religion/pilgrimages;
6. Other.

Theobald (1994) recommends that tourism consumption expenditures should be identified by a system of main categories, and should include:

1. Package travel (holidays and pre-paid tour arrangements);
2. Accommodation (hotels, motels, resorts etc.);
3. Food and drinking establishments;
4. Transport (air, rail, ship, bus, taxi etc.);
5. Recreation, culture and sporting activities;
6. Shopping;
7. Other.

Any demand for tourism should include some form of activity, and yet this important characteristic is seldom assessed. Gilbert (1990) believes that greater

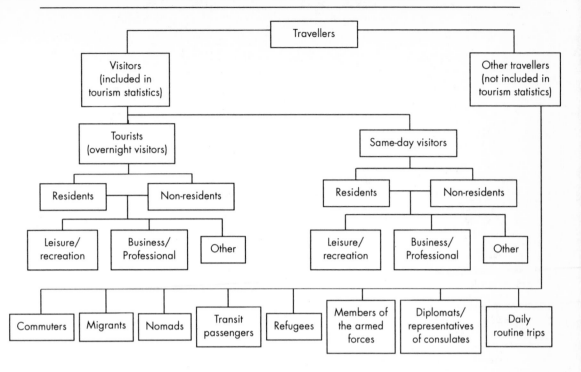

Figure 1.1 Classification of travellers. *Source*: Theobald (1994).

consideration should therefore be given to demand segmentation and activity preferences in the analysis of tourism. Furthermore, if tourism enterprises are to be successful in developing marketing plans, then they need to understand the nature and behaviour of each of the segments they attempt to satisfy. The classification scheme offered by Chadwick (1987) extends the primary purpose of visit to include activities (see Figure 1.2). Gilbert (1990) provides more specific classifications of the main types of activity that represent certain aspects of tourism demand. These he saw as communing with nature; visiting attractions; visiting heritage sites; sports activities, such as skiing; entertainments other than sport; relaxation; health purposes; shopping; and business activities.

While writers differ on the degree to which other forms of travel (e.g. for business, health or educational purposes) should be included under tourism, there is a growing recognition that tourism constitutes one end of a broad leisure spectrum. Gilbert (1990) sees tourism as part of a continuum of activities ranging from local leisure pursuits and home-based activities (non-tourist), to those of travel away from home or work and extended tours (tourist). Defining leisure is just as problematic as defining tourism, but leisure can be thought of as a combined measure of time and attitude of mind to create periods of time when other obligations are at a minimum (Cooper *et al.* 1993). Recreation can be thought of as

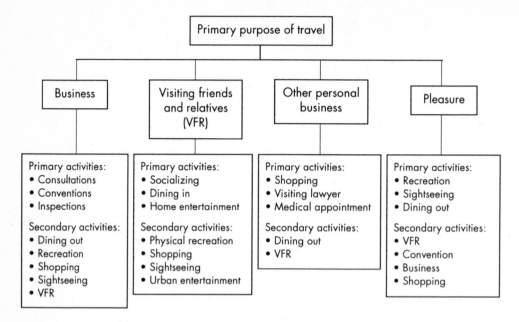

Figure 1.2 Classification of travellers' activities. *Source*: Chadwick (1987).

the pursuits engaged in during leisure time, and an activity spectrum can be identified from recreation around the home, at one end of the scale, through to tourism where an overnight stay is involved, at the other (see Figure 1.3). Cooper *et al.* (1993) classify tourists in two basic ways that relate to the nature of their trip: firstly, the distinction between domestic and international tourists; secondly, the purpose of visit. Within the latter, three categories are cited:

1. Leisure and recreation (including holiday sports and cultural tourism; visiting friends and relatives);
2. Other tourism purposes (including study and health tourism);
3. Business and professional (including meetings, conferences, incentive and business tourism).

Although a minority of skiers do go skiing for purely health or educational purposes, skiing can be placed into the first of these three classifications. In the UK, skiing is often classified as an 'activity holiday', whereas in the United States, it is embraced by the US adventure travel industry. In fact, in the US, skiing is the third most popular adventure activity behind camping and hiking ('The US adventure travel industry' 1997). The author prefers to place skiing in the growing sphere of 'sports tourism'. Sport and tourism tend to be treated by academic and practitioner alike as separate spheres of activity, and integration of the two

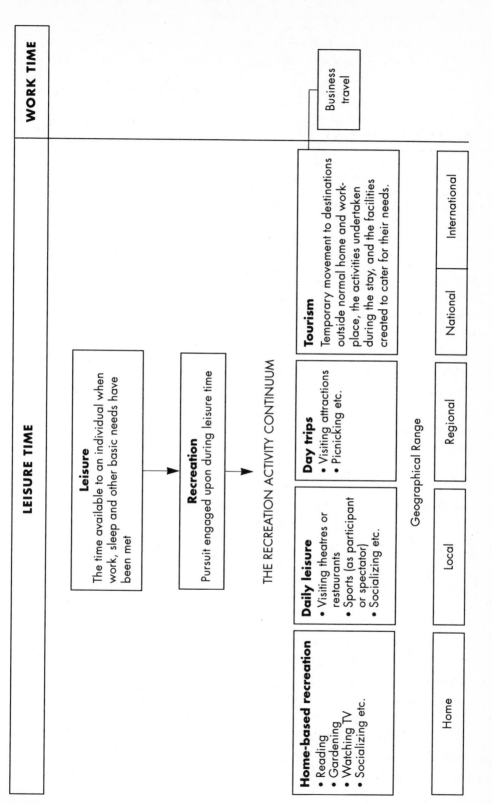

Figure 1.3 Leisure, recreation and tourism. *Source:* Cooper *et al.* (1993).

disciplines is rare. However, in terms of popular participation and some aspects of practice they are inextricably linked (Glyptis 1991). These links have been strengthened in recent years because of several new influences and trends. These include:

1. the common contribution both sport and tourism might make to economic regeneration;
2. the heightened sense of the benefits of exercise for health;
3. the increased stress in the media upon consumer choice of venues;
4. the increased media profile of international sport.

Heineman (1986) has observed that sport is now in many cases a highly structured activity with a production background that is highly technical, and commercially organized and profit-oriented. Sports experiences in the wilds of nature are now so well controlled that they can be efficiently administered and smoothly packaged: created and structured as a particular type of tourist experience. 'Game tourism' in Kenya and 'sports tourism' in the Gambia have become new variants of the widespread pervasion of the 'romantic gaze' (Urry 1990). Likewise, skiing is no longer the strenuous climb to risky terrain and untouched nature, but a mass touristic undertaking in a highly mechanized ski arena. How the activity of skiing has developed into such an important part of sports tourism is described in the next section.

1.2 THE EVOLUTION OF SKIING

Documentation of skiing's earliest emergence as a leisure pastime associated with tourism dates back to the mid-nineteenth century in Europe. There are references to Norwegians travelling on skis from Telemark to Christiana (now Oslo) in Norway, primarily for social purposes, in 1868. Almost two decades later (1890), recreational skiing emerged in North America (Scharff 1974), and soon after this date, socially focused skiing clubs began to develop across Europe and North America. These organizations not only fostered travel between them for socially focused competition, but also facilitated the creation of more and better ski facilities (Batchelor *et al.* 1937). It is believed that winter mountain holidays started after 1866, when a hotelier from St Moritz in Switzerland invited a small group of British summer guests to visit his property during the winter months (Cockerell 1988). They accepted and, once back from their trip, enthused so much about their experience that it became the 'in' thing among the British upper classes to take a winter holiday in Switzerland. In the early days of skiing there were no lifts, and so much time was spent in walking and climbing mountains, but in the winter of

1910–11 Sir Henry Lunn managed to persuade the local authorities in Murren to open the Lauterbrunnen–Murren railway line. The Lauberhorn drag-lift opened the following year. Lunn was also responsible for the first ever downhill race, organized in Montana, Switzerland in 1911. Meanwhile, the 1905 Olympic Games included skiing in its programme of activities despite skiing not being a recognized Olympic event. This inclusion was in response not only to a growing interest in skiing as a participant sport, but also to a desire on the part of the destination's managers and developers to keep the site operational for the entire winter season. In the process of developing this strategy, the concept of a broader set of physical facilities and a more sustainable market base for skiing development is believed to have originated (Williams 1993).

By the beginning of the First World War in 1914 there were at least as many German skiers in Switzerland as there were British. Hotel accommodation was already in good supply, with Switzerland accounting for over 215,000 hotel beds in 1914. Demand was further enhanced as a result of the higher profile that skiing was receiving in potential travel markets (see Figure 1.4). In 1924, skiing was introduced as a formal event at the Olympics in Chamonix, France. It was highlighted again in the 1932 Olympic Winter Games in Lake Placid. These two occurrences helped to place skiing in the forefront of winter recreational activity in both Europe and North America and gave a further push to its development as a major contributor to winter-based tourism (Liebers 1963).

Figure 1.4 Early skiers in the Swiss resort of Verbier.

Few ski resorts had any uphill transport capability specifically for skiers until the 1930s (Williams 1993). The early railways, ratchet trains and buses were used primarily for summer visitors, but a few skiers in resorts like Davos, Zermatt and Wengen took advantage of them to pursue their new sporting pastime. In 1929, the first mechanically propelled uphill lift designed just for skiers was installed in Canada, and within a few years most ski slopes of any significance in North America and Europe had one or more improved versions of it in place. Snow-trains transporting thousands of skiers to the slopes became commonplace throughout North America in the 1930s. In 1936 Union Pacific developed the first tourism-oriented ski resort in Sun Valley, Idaho, and this became the prototype for world-class ski areas in North America.

In Europe, traditional summer Alpine vacation destinations were beginning to recognize the potential of skiing as a source of winter tourists. The first real mountain resort in France was Megeve, its development coinciding with the first ski-lift in France in 1933. Soon after, the Kandahar binding (which replaced the heel strap with a spring loaded cable) was introduced; it was to be the forerunner of the modern skiing technique. The Winter Olympic Games of 1936 held in Parten-kürchen, included both downhill and slalom races. Just as interest in skiing was beginning to quicken, its growth was dampened by the Second World War.

It was not until after the Second World War that skiing in a mass tourism context began to emerge. Skiing demand mushroomed during the post-war period for a number of reasons. Pushed by the military role that skiing played in northern combat areas, skiing was introduced to thousands of returning troops as a form of winter recreation; rapid improvements resulted in safer and more comfortable ski equipment; and better access to ski destinations was brought on by the develop-ment of family automobiles and rising standards of living. By the mid-1940s, skiing had woven its way into the leisure and travel patterns of a strong core of North American and European residents. Skiers began seeking opportunities for longer-stay visits to ski destinations. By the late 1940s and 1950s the second phase of ski resort development took place in France with the opening of centres such as Courcheval, Meribel and Tignes. Along with the availability of on-slope activities for skiing, off-slope amenities for après-skiing became apparent. Ski facilities and services associated with lodging, food, beverages and entertainment became important components of the ski vacation experience (Tanler 1966).

The 1960s saw the start of the great ski boom. Europe witnessed the creation of a new generation of fully integrated ski stations, while in North America, larger resorts in New England, Colorado, California, the Canadian Rockies and the Eastern townships of Quebec emerged to meet the growing demand for winter vacations. Wooden skis and leather boots were slowly phased out and replaced by metal and fibre glass skis and plastic boots. While the 1970s were a period of massive market and product expansion, the 1980s presented a decade characterized by industry consolidation and product management (Williams 1993). Influenced by changing demographics, skiing markets began to mature. By the mid-1980s ski facility supply had in many regions outstripped demand, and many less well-managed ski destinations were experiencing financial difficulties (Kottke 1990). In response, many ski destinations were forced to address both product and market issues in a more business-like fashion, and a more tourism-focused approach to ski area development commenced. Larger ski centres with tourist, rather than primarily resident, ski markets continued to grow, while many small centres faltered. Consequently, between 1980 and 1990 the number of ski areas dropped by 18 per cent in North America. Counteracting this trend, ski area capacity expanded by approximately 51 per cent in the same period.

It is worth noting here the sheer variety of ways to ski. Snowboarding is discussed later on in this chapter, but apart from just sliding downhill (officially termed *Alpine downhill*), one can ski in the following ways: *cross-country skiing*, which is the most ancient way of skiing and requires special long, metal-edged skis allowing skiers to travel horizontally from place to place; *extreme skiing*, which is growing in popularity but is very dangerous, requiring total control and spot-on precision; *heliskiing*, which is skiing via transportation by helicopter; *horse-drawn skiing*, an old tradition in Finland that has yet to take off in the Alps; *mono-skiing*, which is skiing with both feet strapped into one very fat ski; and *ski touring* or *mountaineering*, where participants use special skins on their skis to access mountains not accessible by ski-lifts.

Competitive skiing has come a long way from the first Alpine ski races devised by the British. No-one played a greater part in promoting this new event than Sir Arnold Lunn, who dreamt up the first downhill race in 1911 at Montana in Switzerland. In those days the skiers raced side by side, down wide courses, the first past the flag being the winner. The first safety measure was the abolition of mass-start races in favour of timing contestants who started at one-minute intervals. From the early days of wooden skis and leather boots, there has been fierce rivalry among manufacturers to produce better equipment for the racer. The skis, the waxes and even the clothing are constantly researched and tested – high-tech leotards and helmets are refined these days in wind-tunnels before they are employed on the downhill slopes.

Those responsible for course safety have had to improve the safety netting, and replace the traditional straw bales with foam padding. Today's racers – gliding machines on skis that often reach speeds of 90 mph – reflect the fashion for artificial and over-groomed downhill course settings, where everything is sacrificed to speed and all the jumps and bumps are shaved and flattened in the name of safety. Champions of previous generations were not as muscularly developed and more able to deal with the rolls and bumps of less manicured courses that demanded balance and agility just as much as courage.

There are those who fear that in the years since Lunn started it all, downhill ski racing has become over-groomed, too technical, over-specialized and boring. Lunn himself came to despise what he saw as the artificiality of much modern skiing and suggested that the decline of mountain skiing was closely associated with the development of piste racing.

1.3 ALTERNATIVE WINTER SPORTS

Ski destinations, and in fact the whole ski industry, cannot afford to ignore the active non-skier who still travels to the mountains in the winter. Williams and Dossa (1990) estimate that 20–30 per cent of visitors to ski centres in Canada do not ski. An analysis of market trends in Europe suggests, similarly, that an increasing proportion of those who take winter sports holidays on a regular basis do not ski at all; the respective share among the French, for example, is estimated to be as high as 40 per cent (Cockerell 1994). Even those who do ski are, reportedly, skiing, on average, fewer hours each day than in the past. Wickers (1994) suggests that one in eight visitors to Zermatt, one of Switzerland's top ski resorts, does not ski. Some believe that successful resorts of the future will treat skiing as a form of entertainment; establish more off-slope diversions; reposition themselves to appeal more to women and children; and create a mountain retirement haven for aging 'baby boomers' (Castle 1998).

Many resorts have made significant capital investments in providing alternative activities (Rowan 1989), and these days active non-skiers will find an increasing menu of substitute sports facilities, including heated pools, mini-gyms, saunas and solaria. Most Alpine ski resorts have developed such a wide range of sports and activities to attract *summer* holiday-makers, but the facilities are increasingly used in the winter months. Vail in Colorado has created Adventure Ridge, a four-acre complex at the 10,350 ft level of Vail Mountain, alive with music and featuring a wide choice of restaurants and great range of activities (Best 1997). Adventure Ridge was developed because guest surveys had indicated a lack of evening activities; crowds now often exceed 2000 per night. The outdoor activities range from the high-energy (like snowboarding, ice-skating and the latest craze of 'snowtubing') to the more passive (like a moonlit snowmobile ride). Many ski brochures provide detailed information about facilities – such as tennis halls, snow rafting, skating rinks, horse riding, go-karting, tobogganing, curling and hot-air ballooning – that individual resorts may offer. In Zermatt for example, the 12.5 per cent of visitors who choose not to ski can select from 38 mountain restaurants served by cable-car, chair-lift or funicular. The resort has 30 km of footpaths, sleigh rides along the car-free streets, 15 indoor pools, a curling hall, ice rink, indoor golf, and language courses. Specialist packages now cater for those wishing to take winter walking weeks in the Alps; ride the Cresta Run (bobsleighing) in St Moritz; toboggan in St Anton; or ride a snowmobile (or 'skidoo') in Finland. In addition, there is also the possibility of going ice-climbing or ice-driving, playing ice golf, and even building igloos. Also, 'telemarking' appears to be making a comeback. This old-fashioned skiing technique takes its name from the province of Telemark in south-eastern Norway and is taught by ski schools throughout Scandinavia. Instructors in many alpine resorts and in North America teach it too. The telemark turn, designed to be executed in a loose-heeled binding, and worn with lightweight boots and skis that are comfortable when walking uphill and on the flat, has come into its own again.

Heliskiing

As recently as the mid-1980s, heliskiing was still an elitist pastime with an almost James Bond image. However, the helicopter is simply a very expensive taxi that takes skiers to the best and often the most remote snowfields where – far from the madding crowds – they can enjoy the experience of deep snow. Since the invention of the 'Fat Boys' in the early 1990s, heliskiing has been opened up to a greater cross-section of skiers who might otherwise have never attempted it. Ironically, just as heliskiing became available to the masses, it became less acceptable in a European milieu that was becoming more environmentally aware. Because it is noisy and intrusive, it is technically banned in France and most of Switzerland and Austria.

North America – and particularly Canada – has fewer environmental pressures, largely because there is so much more space. British Columbia is renowned world-wide for its superb heliskiing. USA resorts, not having Canada's vast wilderness areas, don't feature heliskiing to the same degree as the Canadian specialists. Ruby Mountain heliskiing in Nevada claims to be the biggest US operation. Potentially, the Himalayas is the most exciting playground in the world for heliskiers, but the very qualities that make it so exciting – it is remote, vast, untamed, and high – are the factors that have so far delayed its development. Following the collapse of the Soviet Union, a number of new and exotic heliskiing operations have sprung up. The best known is at Guduari, high in the desolate Caucasus, where the Swiss have taken over an operation started by the Austrians in a self-contained, western-style resort hotel, the Sporthotel. New Zealand claims to have more mountains than the Alps, and more heliskiing than anywhere outside Canada. South Island has many options; the best known is Harris Mountain Heliski based in the principal resort towns of Queenstown and Wanaka.

Snowboarding

The sport that is having the greatest impact on the ski industry is snowboarding: it is now probably the biggest winter sport in the USA, and its popularity in Europe is burgeoning (Balmer 1995). Amazingly, there is no single body that compiles statistics on skiing and snowboarding across Europe. There are apparently four million snowboarders worldwide (Newsom 1996). In the USA, the National Ski Association, in conjunction with Ski Industries America, has been plotting the snowboard increase carefully. The USA has some two million snowboarders compared to five million cross-country skiers and ten million alpine skiers. Therefore, in many US resorts, snowboarding represents 20 per cent of lift ticket sales, and this is expected to rise to 30 per cent in the next five years. According to Spring (1996a), the percentage of American people visiting ski destinations who say they snowboard increased in 1996–7 to 27 per cent of the population, up from 15 per cent on the previous season, and from 9 per cent the season before. However, the 1997–8 season saw the first signs of a slowing down in the growth of snowboarding, after three consecutive years of dramatic growth. Statistics show that 29 per cent of downhillers in North America say they are boarders (see Figure 1.5); the growth in snowboarders is attributed to the increased percentage of under 24-year-olds in the market (Spring 1998). In previous years, growth came from cross-over skiers, though the cross-over frenzy among adults has now virtually stopped for all age groups. Spring suggests that, in general, many resorts are reluctant to consider the sport as an opportunity to increase traffic and revenues. Deer Valley and Alta in Utah and Taos in New Mexico still outlaw snowboarders, and in Japan snowboarders are banned from 75 per cent of resorts. Ironically, snowboarding was included in the recent Winter Olympics, held in Nagano, Japan. In Europe, snowboarding is increasing at a slower pace than in North America, and in France boarders make up only 9 per cent of mountain users (Hardy 1997).

The snowboard boom, which has had a greater impact on young people, has caused the ski industry to assess its effect on the market. One of the disadvantages of skiing is that it is technically demanding at a high level of performance. Unless one starts at a very young age, the average recreational skier taking an annual two-week holiday cannot develop the skills necessary to ski steep, fast runs, big bumps and deep powder snow. However, a snowboarder (and the author writes from experience) can learn to stay upright and turn after one morning, and can tackle powder within a week. Such a high learning curve has led to many skiers crossing

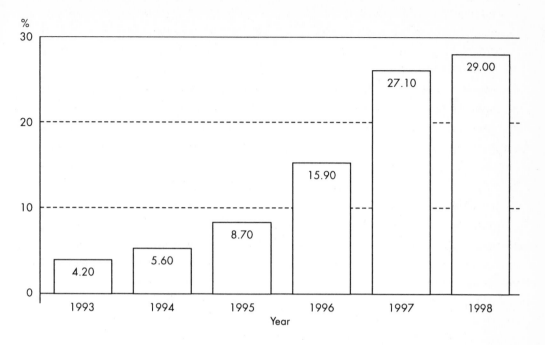

Figure 1.5 Snowboarders as a percentage of downhillers. *Source*: Spring (1998).

over to boarding, and figures from North America indicate that over 60 per cent of boarders have skied before they adopted boarding (Spring 1997).

It is clear that the growth and impulse for innovation in the winter sports business is coming from snowboarding rather than conventional skiing. Projections show that the proportion of mountain users on snowboards may come to be greater than that of conventional skiers within the next ten to twenty years (Scott 1995); some predict that snowboarding could account for a third of winter sports holidays within a few years (Heard 1995). As far as those of school age are concerned, snowboarding is 'in' and skiing has been forgotten. The impact of it being a Winter Olympic sport has enticed thousands of schoolchildren to take to the slopes, and the British Snowboarding Association (BSA) has sent out a sixteen-page information supplement to 6500 secondary schools across the country. The BSA has over 2300 members, 40 per cent of whom are aged under twenty.

Faced with the inevitable rise of snowboarding, both skiers in general and resort authorities in particular, are increasingly conciliatory towards snowboarders and their needs. It is now generally agreed in Europe that adherents of the two disciplines must coexist on the same slopes. Those that believe that snowboarders should be confined to particular mountains or pistes (see Bray 1995) are now a minority. Resorts that practise such discrimination – most of them in North

America – are starting to notice problems in attracting family business. Many resorts in Europe, especially in France, Switzerland and Austria, are making a special effort to attract families with snowboarding children, by building special snowboard parks, complete with half-pipe jumps.

Many ski schools now have special snowboarding sections to ensure that they do not lose custom to some of the newly formed snowboard schools, and an increasing number of potential instructors are studying to gain qualifications to teach snowboarding as well as skiing. Most of the design and fashion innovations in equipment and clothing are heavily influenced by the snowboard culture, and tour operators are also starting to harness the potential of the snowboarding growth. Many are changing the emphasis of their marketing and their range of accommodation. Crystal Holidays were the first major UK operator to produce a brochure directed at snowboarders. They feature a range of dedicated accommodation, tuition and equipment-hire packages. Inghams have a combination ski/snowboard product in four Austrian resorts, where beginners can try both disciplines and decide which is for them. Thomson have just expanded their snowboarding with six specially chosen resorts offering 'Freeriders', a snowboard guiding service. They have 'learn to ride' packages at another thirteen snowboard centres. Finally, Panorama have an emphasis on snowboarding throughout their dedicated Snowboard brochure, and include special snowboard camps. In 1997 they introduced the concept of 'switch packs', allowing skiers and snowboarders to switch between equipment for the different sports for a cost of £57 for six days. However, some operators and many downhill skiers continue to sneer at snowboarding as a passing fad, as inconsequential as the mono-ski. They ignore its popularity at their peril. Increasingly, downhillers are crossing over between the two disciplines, and the evidence presented above suggests significant growth. Also, an estimated 30,000 people attended the Switzerland Snowboard Cup in November 1995, an inaugural event which ran to a packed Covent Garden Plaza, and attracted major sponsorship from Swatch. And in Britain in 1996 some 13,500 pairs of skis and 10,000 snowboards were sold. Significant sales for a fad!

1.4 ARTIFICIAL SKI SLOPES

Skiing on plastic slopes, or dry slopes as they are called, has become a very popular and successful offshoot of skiing. Twenty years ago, skiing on dry ski slopes was virtually unknown: the slopes that did exist were small and only used by enthusiasts practising for snow trips. Now dry slope skiing can be regarded as a sport in its own right, and the 150 or so artificial slopes in the UK are being used by many of Britain's skiers and snowboarders, including beginners, schoolchildren, racers, freestyle skiers and cross-country enthusiasts. The sport's ruling body, the British Ski and Snowboard Federation, actively encourages all its member clubs to use dry slopes to the full.

Before the 1960s, people had been trying for years to find a substitute for snow that could be skied on. There were attempts to ski on beds of pine needles, straw, coconut matting, plastic chips and ice granules. All these failed, mainly because they did not provide the *feel* of snow. It was a ski enthusiast and brush manufacturer called Len Godfrey who developed the first real dry slope in 1961 after discovering that wood (skis) would skate well across brushes. Along with the manager of Simpsons of Piccadilly he produced a mat made of PVC bristles held together by steel bands, and opened Britain's first indoor artificial slope. It was 50 ft by 20 ft (small by today's standards) and was housed in the Philbeach Hall in central London. Mr Godfrey's Dendix skiing surface was marketed under the name of Snowslope; other surfaces – mainly injection-moulded plastics – have since been introduced, offering surfaces for different requirements.

The first outdoor slope was erected at a Torquay holiday camp two years after Godfrey's, and from then on new slopes appeared steadily, most of them connected with ski shops. The first slopes were straightforward up-and-down runs, but as they became used more and more for teaching and training, and then for recreational activities, they became bigger and more ambitious. The best artificial slopes are those that attempt to simulate mountain conditions by varying the slopes and gradients; by having adequate nursery areas that are not too steep to frighten beginners; and that have long run-out areas at the bottom of the slope. The council-run slope at Hillend near Edinburgh is Europe's biggest. It has a 400 m downhill slope, a nursery area, a cross-country section and a large grass skiing area. Hillend teaches tens of thousands of pupils every year, many of them from schools, and also hosts many racing and freestyle contests. Britain boasts many other big, well-run slopes including Pontypool, Gloucester Ski Centre, Ski Rossendale in Lancashire and Wycombe Summit-Abbey in Buckinghamshire. Today, the centrepiece of Britain's artificial ski industry is the Snowdome in Tamworth, Staffordshire, which uses indoor artificial snow to simulate the skiing experience. Critics have suggested that it has the ambience of a meat freezer rather than Alpine charm, and the leisure centre smell of swimming-pool chlorine in place of fresh mountain air. However, the centre has proved to be extremely popular, and was at the centre of a recent launch by the Snowsports Industry of Great Britain, *Snow-Life '98*, which was a bid to bring in new blood by promoting the benefits of artificial venues such as the Snowdome. Snowdome is geared up for beginners, and so they concentrate on giving high-quality lessons. They have also capitalized on the growth of snowboarding by hosting special events, such as snowboard-only Saturday nights, when DJs provide the soundtrack for riders. They also have advanced courses available for improvers in both skiing and snowboarding.

In general terms, the advantages to all skiers of using a dry slope are enormous. The main advantages must be their accessibility and the fact that it is possible to ski all the year round. Regular use of artificial slopes makes virtually obsolete the pre-ski exercises, and training before a ski trip reduces the risk of injury. In a more specific way, skiing on dry ski slopes can be a positive help to skiers of all grades. For beginners, dry slopes offer an easier, quicker, safer and cheaper way of learning basic skills. It also encourages beginners to learn better technique. When the ski travels over, and edges into, the plastic, the matting gives way like snow, yet offers much less resistance to the ski, thus giving the skier more leeway. Because plastic is less slippery than snow, control and turning skills have to be more accurate, and so a better technique is learnt. One spin-off of this is that the beginner often finds it easier to ski on snow than on plastic. Established skiers benefit because skiing faults and bad habits are easier to notice on an artificial slope and it is simpler to isolate a problem and sort it out. Advanced skiers, including racers and freestylers, use the slopes extensively for practice and to achieve perfection.

The future for dry ski slopes is optimistic. British makers are exporting their slopes all over the world, and several private slopes have already been installed in back gardens. An increasing number of schools are including dry slope skiing in their physical education curriculum. If the skiing holiday business is healthy, then potential skiers will continue to give dry slopes a boost by trying out the sport on plastic before committing themselves to hundreds of pounds on a winter sports holiday; for them it is an insurance against spending a lot of money on something they may not like or indeed feel they cannot do.

CONCLUSION

It is commonly believed that current definitions of tourism are not adequate for marketers, since they have been derived for economists. The simplistic view of tourist behaviour could be rejected and replaced with a new understanding of the tourist as a consumer who demonstrates particular forms of behaviour. These involve the needs, motivation, attitudes, values, personality and perceptions that all lead to specific preferences for tourism-related activities.

While writers differ on the degree to which various forms of travel should be included under tourism, there is a growing recognition that tourism constitutes one end of a broad leisure spectrum. Attempts to classify tourism activities have been made, but few authors refer to the growing area of sports tourism, and it is within this category of tourism that the author believes skiing should reside.

Over the last 100 years, skiing has evolved from a niche pastime for the privileged few in Switzerland to a mass international touristic activity. Periods of incredible expansion in the 1970s and 1980s have been followed by problems of overcapacity in both Europe and North America. This maturity of markets has led to considerable consolidation in the industry, and destinations are now developing under strict guidelines and careful control. The impulse for inovation in the ski industry is coming from alternative wintersports, in particular snowboarding, although there is evidence that the growth of this new sport is now slowing down.

CASE STUDY: SKI CLUB OF GREAT BRITAIN

The history of the Ski Club of Great Britain (SCGB) is inexorably bound up with the history of the development of skiing as a sport. In the years before the First World War skiing in the High Alps developed a great deal and became increasingly popular. In 1903 some of the very early pioneers gathered together in London on 6 May for dinner at the Café Royal. They did this for the express purpose of founding an organization that would help to develop downhill skiing in the Alps; improve the style of those enthusiasts who already had some experience; encourage and assist newcomers to the sport; and bring about fraternization among those in any way interested in skiing. This was the birth of the SCGB. At that time such an organization was unique. Now, some 96 years later, it still is. It is perhaps para-doxical how Britons have helped to develop skiing and mountaineering, although Britain lacks adequate mountains for both sports.

The Club magazine was started in 1905 and remains a fascinating record of the changes over the years in equipment, clothes, facilities (such as ski-lifts), the technique of skiing, and holidays. In early volumes there are references to reaching resorts by horse-drawn sleighs, pictures of ladies skiing in skirts, and reports of races where all the competitors started at the same time down untracked slopes. Very early on, in 1905, the SCGB introduced the first system of ski tests, with first-, second- and third-class badge awards. These tests were the first downhill ski tests ever devised and they were widely copied. Today there is no nation and virtually no ski resort that does not have similar tests. However, before the 1914–18 war, the SCGB concentrated on cross-country skiing, and the first official British ski championships at Saanenmoser, Switzerland, were awarded on the combined result of a cross-country race and a jumping competition. It was not until 1920 that a championship held in Wengen, Switzerland, included a 'style' competition and a downhill race. At this time, British skiers were persuading the Swiss to open the railways they used for summer walkers in places like Zermatt, Wengen and Murren. These, in fact, became the very first ski-lifts.

Figure 1.6 A Ski Club leader with a party in Zermatt.

The period 1920–39 has become known as the golden age of British skiing. In 1922, Arnold Lunn, the Club's great ski pioneer, set the first modern slalom on the slopes of Murren. He always preferred racers to set off on his courses without studying them first – a true test of skiing in natural conditions. In January 1924 a few inspired members of the SCGB, vastly intrigued by the thrills and future possibilities of early downhill races, came together in Murren and founded the Kandahar Ski Club. The Kandahar was the first organization to be formed with the express purpose of promoting the two events that came to be known as the Alpine disciplines, downhill and slalom, as opposed to the long-standing Nordic disciplines of cross country and jumping. This growing competitive spirit prompted the establishment of the Fédération Internationale de Ski (FIS) in 1924. In that year, the first winter Olympic Games were held, although they covered Nordic events only. By 1928 – the year of the second Olympic Games in St Moritz – the FIS had recognized the SCGB's rules for downhill and slalom races. A Canadian ski team took part at St Moritz, and the third games were held in the USA at Lake Placid. However it was during the fourth Winter Games in Garmisch-Partenkirchen in 1936 that the modern event took on its recognizable appearance with the inclusion of downhill and slalom races, run on SCGB rules. It was about this time, too, that the first significant steps were being made with equipment. The SCGB's technical committee was responsible for the introduction of the first safety release strap, and the first metal edges appeared. After the Second World War the development of equipment continued with the introduction of metal skis and then, in the 1960s, of fibreglass compounds.

By the end of the 1940s, the SCGB had representatives in the Alps. The numbers of British skiers were rising each year, and it was the representatives' role to take these members around the resorts. Having started in a small way, the Club now (1998–9) has reps in 37 resorts on both sides of the Atlantic; they look after the interests and activities of members on the snow and provide the press with accurate and unbiased snow reports. The SCGB organizes an annual representatives' course in the Alps in order to train and select suitable, qualified people. Because the SCGB has been such a force in recreational skiing, it has a good long-standing relationship with a large number of resorts. The resorts usually host the representatives for the winter season.

Another facility provided by the Club for its members is the organization of ski parties. Touring parties were first organized in the 1930s and, although the boom in mass travel fuelled by the introduction of charter flights increased the competition, the Club's skiing parties continued to grow. They tended to provide for specific needs: for instance, parents could send their children on their own, and go elsewhere to learn to ski in powder. All the parties had leaders (see Figure 1.6) who acted as guides on the slopes and generally ensured that the clients had an enjoyable skiing holiday. The formula is the same today, and fills a gap in the skiing market that cannot be bridged by mass tour operators.

In 1964 the Club decided that too much of the money it collected from members in subscriptions was going to keep the Alpine and cross-country racing teams operating. So, at a historic meeting the National Ski Federation of Great Britain (now the British Ski and Snowboard Federation) was set up as a governing body of skiing in Great Britain. The Ski Club retained responsibility for recreational skiers while the BSF took over the funding and organization of ski racing. For many years the two organizations shared the same premises in Eaton Square, London, until the 1980s when the BSF moved its offices to Scotland. The Ski Club has now moved to a new freehold clubhouse in the centre of Wimbledon Village. The Club continues to flourish, and is involved in numerous activities apart from the Club holidays and the representative service. An important resource is its information department: members can telephone or come in to ask which resort will suit their kind of skiing. The department collects snow reports during the skiing season, distributes them to the national newspapers, and runs a special telephone line that anyone can call to find out detailed information about skiing conditions in any resort. The modern version of the Club's magazine is different from the original small, blue annual, and is now a colourful A4-sized magazine. It was, in 1972, initially called *Ski Survey*; in 1997 it became *Ski and Board*. Published five times a year, it concentrates on giving members both information and entertainment. The magazine is free to members and is also sold in bookshops. Circulation in 1998–9 was 17,500.

Recent developments in Britain, with which the SCGB has been associated, are the growth in the number of artificial slopes and the popularity of grass skiing. The dry slope boom has resulted in the construction of about 150 slopes around the UK, and the SCGB arranges year-round courses on many of these artificial slopes. The Club also organizes social events for members, as well as guest lectures on skiing-related subjects. Members can also take advantage of substantial discounts on anything from holidays, to year-round insurance, to equipment in the resort. A joint venture with Thomas Cook Direct allows members to book holidays with major tour operators, at a discount. The Club also organizes publicity events in resorts. One example is the Verbier Challenge Cup held every Easter in Verbier, Switzerland. The race is a giant slalom open to all, and in 1998 a record 230 competitors of all nationalities entered the race. It is sponsored by local businesses, and over 80 prizes were awarded for 24 categories that included different standards, local workers, professional racers, ski guides, snowboarders, and children. The Challenge Cup is awarded to the fastest family, but there are numerous booby prizes, including the 'best fall' which in 1996 went to Ian Botham!

The current mission statement for the Club is 'to become the high-profile organization that all skiers belong to, by providing high-quality services, promoting safe, fun skiing and snowboarding for all standards, *and* offering excellent value' (see Taylor 1997, Section 1.2). Objectives in the short term are to increase the profile of the Club, and to improve the image so as to attract a wider range of people to the Club. The Club is aware that its image has been old-fashioned for quite some time, but it is beginning to appeal to the new generation of skiers and snow boarders. It is also seeking to improve services to members, with the aim of retaining existing members, and attracting new members. In 1998, the Club had 14,279 members (24,000 including members of families) – which is approximately 3 per cent of the skiing market – who pay annual subscriptions of £45 for an individual, £66 for family and £10 for under 24s. Membership statistics are provided in Appendix 1.1 and a member profile can be found in Appendix 1.2 (see page 24).

The Club policy is decided by an elected council of twelve members. They are volunteers who meet monthly to receive management reports and accounts from the managing and finance directors. Council members' term of office is three years; the president, chairman and treasurer often hold office longer, and are re-elected at the AGM. The Club's rules require the council to prepare financial statements each year; a five-year record is shown in Appendix 1.3 (see page 25). The surplus for 1997 was £405,897, split between £62,014 from revenue operations and £343,883 from the disposal of the Eaton Square premises. In 1998, the Club's assets were close to £1,700,000.

For the long term, the Club believes that an increase in membership will allow it to develop relationships and become an important cog in the ski industry – even the spokesbody for the industry – working with other organizations to promote the sport. It intends to develop its high-quality services, provide better value for existing members, and attract a bigger sector of the ski and snowboard markets. After over 90 years of existence, the Ski Club of Great Britain can look back and see how it has encouraged millions of Britons to ski and, ensured that they enjoy the experience. In an increasingly competitive environment the Club has been forced into adopting a more market-focused approach to its operations. The future is uncertain, but undoubtedly the Club will be celebrating its centenary in 2003 with some style.

Appendices

1.1 Ski Club of Great Britain membership statistics 1977–97.

Date	Membership numbers	Change (%)
1977	13 031	–10
1978	10 323	–20.8
1979	9 420	–8.7
1980	10 110	7
1981	11 360	12.3
1982	12 650	11.3
1984	12 351	–2.4
1985	13 000	5
1986	12 168	–6
1987	13 500	11
1988	14 000	3.7
1989	15 020	7.3
1990	15 796	5
1991	15 969	1.1
1992	15 395	–3.6
1993	14 994	–2.6
1994	14 851	–1
1995	14 995	1
1996	14 153	–5.6
1997	13 607	–3.8

1.2 Ski Club member profile.

	Sex		Income		Skiing
62%	Male	31%	£30–50 000	71%	Intermediate/ Advanced- intermediate
		25%	over £50 000	24%	Expert

	Age		Children		Frequency
51%	25–44 years	69%	no children in household	95%	ski at least once a year
23%	45–54 years			54%	ski two or three times a year
17%	over 55 years				

1.3 Ski Club five-year financial record

	1994	1995	1996 £000s	1997	1998
Income					
Subscription and affiliation fees	535	586	609	621	629
Net income on Club Holiday	22	10	7	18	36
Net income on Fresh Tracks	N/A	N/A	N/A	4	6
Net cost of Ski Survey	(70)	(64)	(76)	(90)	(90)
Bar, catering and functions	6	8	5	1	(2)
Other income	85	94	92	83	131
Surplus on disposal of property	0	0	0	344	0
Total	578	634	637	981	710
Expenditure					
Skiing operations	69	89	95	89	109
Administration, marketing and membership support	343	361	398	400	424
Premises	68	79	59	76	72
Exceptional expenditure (income)	(3) 477	0 529	0 552	0 565	0 605
Surplus (deficit) before taxation	101	105	85	416	105
Corporation tax	(4)	(7)	(10)	(10)	(12)
Surplus after taxation	97	98	75	406	93
Members' fund	1071	1169	1244	1650	1743

[Bracketed figures indicate negatives.]

CHAPTER 2

The World
Ski Market

INTRODUCTION

This chapter provides statistics on the market for winter sports holidays worldwide. Although the USA and Japan account for a high percentage of skiers, there are many options available to skiers in terms of destinations. A profile of these destinations follows, along with a review of the market for clothing and equipment.

2.1 MARKET SIZE

The current ski market is estimated at some 65–70 million skiers worldwide (Cockerell 1994). Around 55 million are primarily downhill skiers, while the remainder prefer cross-country skiing. Neither market nor destination share is easy to determine accurately as there is a dearth of statistical data, and different countries' estimates conflict quite strongly. But Europe accounts for approximately 30 million skiers, including domestic business (those who ski only within the frontiers of their own country). Table 2.1 shows the estimated number of skiers. It should be noted that skiers can make several trips each year, which is why the National Ski Areas Association has figures of 52.7 million for ski visits to US resorts in 1994–5, a drop of 3.6 per cent on the previous year (Goeldner 1996). Germany heads the list of European markets, with some 5.5 million skiers, and is followed by France and Scandinavia with around 5 million each. Much of this ski business is not only domestic, but also involves no overnight stays. The USA and Canada between them generate an estimated 20 million skiers – again primarily domestic – and Japan 14 million. Fewer than one million Americans have ever been abroad for a skiing holiday, and some 400,000 of such trips were to Europe. The number of Japanese people skiing outside Japan is said to be a mere 50,000; Europe has seen about 7500 of them and this number is increasing.

Table 2.1 The world's leading ski markets, 1993. *Source*: Cockerell (1994).

Market	Estimated number of skiers (000s)
USA	15 000
Japan	14 000
Germany	5 500
Canada	5 000
France	5 000
Scandinavia	5 000
Austria	3 000
Italy	3 000
Mexico	2 900
Switzerland	2 000
(United Kingdom	700)

Lazard (1996) has produced a recent report analysing skiing worldwide in terms of countries' resorts, lift numbers and skier visits. The results are shown in Table 2.2. Although Lazard admits that the data presented in the table are imperfect and were not developed for publishing, the figures are unique and offer additional interest when compared to other information. For example, Japan represents over 19 per cent of the world ski area activity, but consumes almost twice this amount in skier equipment; the USA has 14 per cent of the market and accounts for 24 per cent of equipment sales. Lazard believes that the skiing market is mature in Europe as well as in Japan and North America, and is bound to evolve faster in other areas of the world such as eastern Europe, Korea and southeast Asia. According to the latest Mountain International Opinion Survey (MINOS), conducted at ski resorts in Austria, Switzerland, Italy and France, the evidence is that skiing numbers are dwindling in Europe (Spring 1996a). While the average number of *days* skied are up, the actual *number* of skiers is down. The fear is that the vacation skier (from northern countries such as Germany, the Benelux countries, the UK and Scandinavia), who represents half the skier market for the European Alpine countries, is skiing less often.

Figures available in the UK also reflect a maturing industry. Skiing holidays have fallen in line with the total winter holiday market since the recession took hold in the early 1990s; yet, unlike winter holidays, they have not picked up significantly in volume since then. Again, statistics are varied and hard to come by. Mintel (1994, 1996) believe the market to have peaked in 1988–9 with a record 710,000 skiing holidays sold, whereas a Ski Industry Report written by one of the leading operators

Table 2.2 Skiing worldwide. *Source*: Lazard (1996).

Country	Resorts	Lifts	Skier visits	
			million	%
Japan	700	3 600	75	19.2
France	431	4 143	56	14.4
USA	516	2 269	54	13.9
Austria	550	3 473	43	11.0
Italy	260	2 854	37	9.5
Switzerland	480	1 762	31	8.0
Canada	245	1 375	22	5.6
Germany	225	1 670	20	5.1
Sweden	340	950	12	3.1
Norway	210	405	8	2.1
Czechoslovakia (former)	300	1 500	4.8	1.2
Spain	27	294	4.3	1.1
Yugoslavia (former)	21	200	3.0	0.77
Australia	11	139	2.6	0.67
Finland	117	505	2.0	0.51
Poland	15	110	2.0	0.51
South Korea	9	70	1.9	0.49
Andorra	11	115	1.5	0.38
New Zealand	12	64	1.1	0.28
USSR (former)	10	32	0.9	0.23
Chile	14	84	0.8	0.21
Argentina	15	72	0.7	0.18
Bulgaria	7	50	0.6	0.15
Iran	7	45	0.5	0.13
Greece	10	40	0.4	0.10
Turkey	10	25	0.3	0.08
Lebanon	4	18	0.2	0.05
Rest of the world	50	150	2.0	0.50
Total	4 500	26 000	390	100

(Crystal Holidays, 1996) suggests that the total ski market for 1995–6 was 760,000, a slight increase of 2 per cent on the previous year. Their Ski Industry Report on the 1996–7 season was even more encouraging, suggesting that the total skier market had risen to 830,000 skiers. A. C. Nielsen, who compile statistics based on a sample survey of travel agents, suggest that the total number of package skiing holidays booked through agents has risen slowly over the last four years to reach just over 350,000 for the 1997–8 ski season (see Table 2.3). This represented 9.3 per cent of total package holidays sold in that period.

Table 2.3 Package ski holidays sold relative to total package holidays. *Source*: A. C. Nielsen (1998).

Year	Total Holidays	Ski Holidays	Ski Holidays as % of Total Holidays
Winter 1994–5	3 201 420	277 892	8.7
Winter 1995–6	3 330 725	283 217	8.5
Winter 1996–7	3 532 735	319 990	9.1
Winter 1997–8	3 810 308	354 441	9.3

According to Lewis and Wild (1995), the total ski market in the UK consists of about 7.5 million people who have skied at some time, of whom 3.75 million have skied in the past five years. To put the skiing market in context, UK residents made around 42 million visits abroad in 1995, of which 15 million were inclusive tour holidays. Skiing, therefore, has a 4–5 per cent share of the outbound holiday market and a 12 per cent share of the winter holiday market. Other winter segments include winter sun breaks, cruises and lakes and mountain tourism.

Whichever report one acknowledges, the ski market has been fairly flat for five or six years with tour operator sales levelling out at somewhere between 350,000 and 450,000 – almost exactly where the market was a decade ago. A further 150,000–200,000 skiers make their own way to the mountains. The biggest decline has been felt by the specialist schools' skiing operators. Here there has been a dramatic fall from as many as 500,000 ski holidays sold six years ago to as few as 150,000 last season, largely as a result of the 1988 Education Reform Act with its tough regulations for school trips. The consequences, if not addressed, could be considerable, for it is through school trips that many adults acquire their taste for skiing (Balmer 1995), and there is evidence to suggest that many school children consequently introduce their parents to the sport (Mintel 1994).

How much the ski industry is worth worldwide is difficult to gauge. Statistics provided by the National Ski Areas Association (Hager 1989) indicate in excess of $3 billion in annual revenues for US resorts, split between sales of lift tickets and ski shops. Table 2.4 shows Mintel's estimates of the number of skiing holidays taken abroad by the British and the level of expenditure (Mintel 1996). Their figures have been revised from the previous report of 1994, perhaps because of a recognition of the differences between their estimates and those of the industry (and perhaps indicating that their statistics are not always accurate!). Nonetheless, they still suggest a top figure of 645,000 skiers for 1997 compared to 830,000 put forward by Crystal (Crystal Holidays 1997). Note that they are no longer skiing holidays, but 'snow sports' holidays.

Table 2.4 UK snow sports holidays, 1988/9 to 1995/6. *Source*: Mintel (1996).

Year	Holidays (000s)	Index	£ m	Index	Spend per holiday(£)
1988–9	710	100	215	100	303
1989–90	675	95	202	94	299
1990–1	610	86	185	86	303
1991–2	635	89	208	97	328
1992–3	616	87	205	95	333
1993–4	635	89	220	102	346
1994–5	625	88	225	105	360
1995–6	645	91	245	114	380

2.2 DESTINATION PROFILE

United States of America

Skiing in the USA is different from skiing in Europe in many ways. Many of these differences are positive: there is an abundance of snow, and nearly all the resorts have extensive snow-making facilities; the snow grooming is immaculate; the service is friendly and efficient, and most resorts have free guided tours of the mountain; lift queues are rare and well organized; the tree-line often goes right to the top of the mountain; and the accommodation is much more spacious and luxurious than the European equivalent. However, the effects of jet lag and altitude, combined with the length of flight, can be a major deterrent for many Europeans. Also, some find the scenery less attractive than the Alps, with resorts lacking Alpine charm and atmosphere. Most of the mountain restaurants are huge self-service places with little character or culinary pretensions.

Despite these drawbacks, sales to the USA have performed well in the 1990s. During the 1997–8 ski season, about 70,000 Britons took transatlantic flights in order to ski; this accounts for almost 15 per cent of all skiing holidays sold in the UK. Tour operator sales to the USA alone accounted for 20,000 holidays, an increase of nearly 100 per cent on the previous season. Resorts in the United States feature prominently in all the principal tour operators' programmes and there are even a few specialist companies that deal exclusively in North American ski trips. Research indicates that UK skiers visiting the USA are experienced skiers with high disposable incomes who are willing to spend up to four times as much as the average skier to enjoy 'guaranteed' good skiing (Colorado Board of Tourism 1992). Several things happened to make the international – especially the British – business come alive in the USA: several consecutive seasons of poor snow conditions in the Alps encouraged dedicated skiers to look for other destinations; the currency exchange rate improved, making an American ski holiday more competitively priced; and the incredible exposure generated by the World Championships at Vail in 1989 showed off American ski conditions at their finest (Gillen and Best 1991). Moreover, years of marketing evangelism from Ski USA, Colorado Ski Country and major USA destinations such as Snowbird and Jackson Hole began to attract converts.

Skiing in the USA is concentrated in a few main areas. Nearly three-quarters of British skiers going to North America go to Colorado (Mintel 1994), with Breckenridge being the number one choice of resort. Aspen, Vail, Keystone and Steamboat are the other main resorts in Colorado. Skiing in Utah is generally confined to the resorts of Snowbird, Solitude, Park City and Deer Valley, while California boasts the resorts around Lake Taho such as Squaw Valley and Heavenly, as well as Mammoth Mountain further south. Jackson Hole is a popular ski resort in Wyoming, as is Sun Valley in Idaho. In New England, on the East Coast of the USA, Killington and Stowe are probably the best known resorts; Sugarbush, Smuggler's Notch and Sunday River are also successful destinations.

Canada

Canada has reaped huge rewards from its decision to go on the offensive and promote its skiing on price: the number of Britons skiing there now numbers nearly 30,000 – 8.3 per cent of the tour operator market. Sales have been increasing year on year, and the weak Canadian dollar, and direct scheduled services, have seen resorts like Whistler/Blackcomb (two hours' drive north of Vancouver) and Banff/Lake Louise (an hour's drive west of Calgary) increase the number of British visitors by 100 per cent in three years.

Standards in the USA and Canada are incomparably higher than in Europe, and the attitude of staff is warm and friendly (Hardy 1994). The root of this lies in the fact that, with rare exception, each resort and lift system is owned by one company. Everyone, from the ski-shop attendant to ski instructor, works for the same organization with a single corporate identity. By contrast, ownership of the slopes in traditional Alpine resorts may be split between a dozen small farmers. This means a whole range of lift companies, ski schools, ski buses and other services all exist independently of each other in a village usually spiced by generations of inter-family rivalry.

Japan

Table 2.2 on page 28 indicates that Japan represents over 19 per cent of the world ski area activity with 700 resorts and 3600 lifts. Shiga Kogen is Japan's biggest single-ticket resort, consisting of 21 ski areas and incorporating 74 lifts over six mountains. In Japan there are no lift queues. Each time a new lift is built, the old one is left in place. So instead of lift queues there are crowded pistes, full of company employees who are identically dressed and emblazoned with their company names. They ski in tight groups, even though they have widely differing abilities. The resorts are geared towards weekend skiers from the cities, and during the week the slopes are fairly empty. Snowboarders are still not accepted in many Japanese resorts, and, if they are, they are confined to small sectors of the ski area.

Europe

The literature on ski-field development is heavily oriented towards studies from the European Alps, the world's most developed Alpine region in terms of skiing. Barbier (1978) calculated that in 1975–6 about 60 per cent of the world's 20,000 ski-lifts were located in the European Alps. The major developed ski areas of Europe are shared by the five nations of the Alpine arc: France, Italy, Austria, Switzerland and Germany (Lewis and Wild 1995). Together they provide an area of approximately 5800 km^2 of posted and managed skiing (see Table 2.5). The range of destinations visited by UK skiers has expanded rapidly as the market has grown, and as skiers have begun to seek new challenges and experiences (see Table 2.6). Although Austria and France continue to dominate the market, there has been considerable growth in less traditional ski destinations, most notably Andorra and Bulgaria. The three most popular European ski resorts for British skiers in 1997 were Sauze d'Oulx, Italy (11,221 skiers), Livigno, Italy (10,287), and Courcheval, France (7,417). A. C. Nielsen have different statistics from those of Crystal Holidays; they suggest that Italy now has 19 per cent of the market, Austria only 16 per cent and Andorra 12 per cent of the UK market (Lewis 1997). Table 2.7 indicates the changes in destination preference for British skiers over the last four winters. Once

Table 2.5 Major ski areas of Europe. *Source*: Lewis and Wild (1995).

Country	Ski area (km²)
France	2 000
Italy	1 350
Austria	1 050
Switzerland	950
Germany	450

Table 2.6 Total tour operator mix by country 1996–7. *Source*: Crystal Holidays (1997).

Destination	% share of skiers
France	24.5
Austria	20.1
Italy	19.8
USA/Canada	10.6
Bulgaria	8.3
Switzerland	5.0
Others	11.7

Table 2.7 Destination preferences for British skiers. *Source*: A. C. Nielsen (1998).

Destination	Ski Holidays 1994–5 000s	%	1995–6 000s	%	1996–7 000s	%	1997–8 000s	%
France	87	31	77	27	80	25	90	26
Italy	38	13	53	18	65	20	67	19
Austria	72	26	61	22	49	15	56	16
Andorra	18	7	22	8	37	12	41	12
Canada	N/A		N/A		25	8	29	8
USA	N/A		N/A		12	4	20	6
Bulgaria	13	5	15	5	21	7	18	5
Switzerland	33	12	18	7	16	5	17	5

again, these are solely package holidays sold through travel agents, and do not include the independent and schools' market. Austria and Switzerland show significant falls in popularity (26 per cent to 16 per cent, and 12 per cent to 5 per cent of the market, respectively), while Andorra and North America have witnessed significant gains.

The following section profiles the main skiing destinations in Europe.

Austria

Austria has mainly small and mid-size ski centres. Their charm has traditionally made Austria the leading destination for British skiers, but unfavourable exchange rates against a strong Austrian schilling, have resulted in a dramatic drop in traffic. Austria's share has dropped from 50 per cent to 16–20 per cent over the past eight years, despite many hoteliers holding prices for the three seasons, and, in some cases, dropping prices for the British market by as much as 15 per cent ('Ski preview' 1996).

France

Winter sports have enjoyed steady progress in France for the last 25 years, but remain in a state of flux and uncertainty. Despite losing 3.4 per cent of the British market in 1996, France has proved very popular over the last five years, owing to the trend towards self-drive skiing holidays, and the opening of the channel tunnel. The French Alps are the closest world-class ski area to Britain and there is a huge choice of routes and modes of transport. The French also understand that the British often take family holidays for mixed ability groups and, accordingly provide plenty of skiing for all standards of skier in most of its mainstream resorts. In addition, French ski stations positively welcome, rather than simply tolerate, snowboarders and most of them have now built special snowboard parks and are constantly improving their facilities for boarders (Scott 1998). However, the French are worried about the recent drop in numbers, and fear that their product is out of date. For many, the size, facilities and general disposition of French apartments are no longer acceptable. Value comparisons with condominiums in North America make the French product look outmoded, over-priced and uninviting. Nonetheless, for good British skiers, France is likely to remain the most popular country simply because of the quality of its principal ski areas and lift systems.

Switzerland

No-one denies the downturn in the Swiss ski business: the destination that used to sell on quality has become complacent in its service delivery (Hudson and Shephard 1998). Switzerland, with its strong currency and few economies to offer the skier, saw the number of British visitors fall by 200 per cent between 1991 and 1996 (from a 15 per cent share in 1992 to 5 per cent in 1996). Tour operators are confident that those with money will still go to Switzerland, and Swiss tourist officials say the British will quickly return once they sample the inferior quality of a ski holiday in Italy (English 1996). The sense of Swiss tradition and heritage does attract British skiers, and the majority of the ski destinations in Switzerland are old villages that were well established before skiing evolved. Consequently, unlike the situation in France, the development of buildings and ski-lifts has always been strictly controlled (see the case study of Verbier at the end of this chapter).

It does seem that after years of complacency, Switzerland has at last become alert to its shrinking share of the ski market. Few resorts increased their lift-pass prices last year, and Verbier actually reduced its full area one-day ticket and introduced a cheaper pass covering all but the most challenging slopes. The strongest incentive for the British to return to Switzerland is likely to be the exchange rate; the 1997–8 skiing season saw a dramatic improvement in the Swiss market with the pound over 25 per cent stronger against the Swiss franc than it had been in the previous two seasons.

Italy

Owing to sterling's strength against the devalued Italian lira, skiing holidays to Italy have been given a major boost and now account for nearly 20 per cent of the UK market, an increase of over 100 per cent in two seasons. Most of the mass-market operators virtually sold out their Italian programmes at full brochure price in 1996, and expanded considerably the following year. The Italians have invested substantially in their infrastructure over the past few years, and it is only lack of capacity that could hold back their growth. However, the Italian lira has strengthened recently, many Italian resorts have increased their lift-pass prices; and hoteliers are putting up their rates in what they feel is a seller's market. So, although Italy still represents good value, it is no longer the bargain it was.

Spain

One country that is quietly building its ski business is Spain. Although the destination is the second most mountainous in Europe, Spain is usually associated with sunshine holidays. This image has slowed Spain's progress in the winter sports market, although each year more UK operators feature Spain. Sierra Nevada – the most southerly ski resort in Europe – was originally called Sol y Nieve (sun and snow) and its blend of skiing plus easy access to Granada and the hotspots of the Costa del Sol gives it perennial appeal to skiers who prefer sangría, paella and siestas to fondues and Glühwein. The resorts also appeal to non-fanatics in search of a sunny winter holiday where skiing is available but not the only activity. Though Spain has other resorts in the Pyrenees – the small learn-to-ski destinations of Formigal and La Molina, and the up-market, more challenging Baqueira-Beret – only Sierra Nevada and Formigal are making a serious impact on the UK market.

Andorra

Andorra is now taken seriously by most of the major operators and they feature the destination heavily. Built on budget-priced products, the principality's popularity has grown steadily and now boasts five ski areas that have had excellent snow cover over the last few winters. Its market share is difficult to interpret, as Mintel include the country as part of France, but some reports put Andorra's share of UK ski business as high as 12 per cent (Lewis 1997).

Eastern Europe

In Eastern Europe, Bulgaria and Rumania continue to attract groups and first-time skiers. The currency remains relatively weak in both countries but internal costs have risen steadily (Heard 1996). However, both countries remain extremely good value for money and repeat business is high, particularly among families and mixed-ability groups. If the Polish resort of Zakopane in the Tatra Mountains is successful with its bid to stage the Winter Olympics in 2006, the spin-off for the rest of Eastern Europe would be beneficial: long overdue acknowledgement of the investment now being made in the ski product would be certain to fuel operator interest. Increased numbers visiting the mountains of Poland, the Czech Republic, Slovakia, Slovenia, Rumania and Bulgaria would provide funds to raise the quality of these resorts.

Scandinavia

Scandinavia is attracting more skiers every year. Sweden, for example, welcomed 1200 UK skiers in the 1996–7 season, and numbers are expected to increase dramatically since the start of winter charter flights in December 1997. There are around 20–30 ski resorts in Sweden and seven are offered by UK operators (including Crystal and Ski Scandinavia). Are and Salem are the most popular resorts; the former is offering cash back to beginners who cannot master the sport within a week.

Many operators also offer packages to Norway. Its distinct advantage over the Alps is its variety of terrain for cross-country skiing. The Lillehammer Olympics in 1994 provided a boost to the Norwegian ski industry, and despite the cost of alcohol, the skiing is reportedly good value for money. The low temperatures and the northerly latitudes – the main resorts are as far north as Shetland and

Anchorage – mean the skiing season lasts longer than in the rest of Europe. Geilo is the best known resort, and there is also good skiing at Hemsedal, Lillehammer and Voss.

Scotland

Until recently, Scottish skiing, which began in the early 1960s, grew steadily. There are five Scottish ski centres offering 117 ski runs: in the Nevis range and Glencoe (west Scotland), and at Glenshee, Cairngorm and the Lecht (in the east). According to the Scottish Ski Areas Association, the five resorts have averaged 500,000 ski days annually over the last ten years and the Association forecasts that this will increase after the current investment programmes takes effect. These include a £20 million investment at Cairngorm; £7 million spent on the Nevis range area since 1991; and European development fund assistance for the Lecht. The Scottish Tourist Board, together with other public agencies, encourage the development of skiing in the Highlands. In conjunction with A. T. Mays, the largest Scottish travel agent, a Ski Scotland brochure has been produced for the last two seasons. Aviemore is the most famous resort in Scotland; new roads and the installation of chair-lifts have transformed it from the quiet Speyside village of twenty years ago to a year-round activity area.

The skiing industry is vital to the Highlands, each year employing up to 3000 people and injecting more than £30 million into the local economy. Operators have tackled the problem of under-investment but the vagaries of the weather remain. Some now fear that global warming threatens the future of the entire industry (Arlidge 1996). Scotland is still in the back of Britons' thoughts when it comes to choosing a winter sports resort. Lack of awareness is one problem, but the uncertain weather conditions remain the biggest constraint. Scotland generally provides greater enjoyment for experienced skiers since the variable weather means that perfect conditions are rare.

Rest of the world

As for the rest of the world, many of the resorts in Chile, Argentina, New Zealand and even Australia have a strong curiosity value and compelling scenery but sometimes little in the way of challenging skiing (Wilson 1996). It is relatively easy to book a skiing holiday to these countries, and some operators are even offering skiing trips to unusual destinations such as India and Alaska. Japanese skiers who try the slopes at the Japanese-owned resort of Alyeska, the main ski area in Alaska, are astonished by how much space there is. India boasts kilometres of untracked pistes in its resorts of Gulmarg in Kashmir, Auli in Uttar Pradesh, and Kufri, Narkanda, Manali and Rohtang in Himachal. Skiing is also increasingly popular in South Korea where the main resorts of Dragon Valley and Muju are only one hour from Seoul. However, between them, these destinations comprise a very small percentage of the total skiing market.

In retrospect, the trends in destination preferences for British skiers send out confusing messages. On the one hand, there is a huge increase in the numbers travelling to Italy because of price. On the other, it is significant that more expensive and time-consuming skiing holidays to North America should be so buoyant. It would appear that many people are taking a fresh look at what they want from a skiing holiday, but that overall they are seeking value for money.

2.3 SKI CLOTHING AND EQUIPMENT

The market size for ski clothing, equipment and accessories is largely determined by the fortunes of the skiing holiday market, and so sales have suffered over the last decade. To some extent, ski clothing can double up as winter clothing, and so this has provided some protection against falling sales. It has been the equipment market that has experienced the worst effects of the maturing ski industry. Table 2.8 illustrates sales in the UK market from 1990 to 1994. The whole market has fallen from £76.1 million in 1990–1 to an estimated £54.1 million in 1993–4, and all sectors have suffered a decline. One of the reasons for the decline in equipment sales is the improved quality of hired facilities in European resorts. Many skiers now prefer to hire equipment rather than buy their own, and it avoids the problems of travelling with skis, as airlines now charge extra for ski carriage. Poor snow cover in the early 1990s began a trend amongst those with their own equipment to replace it far less frequently than in the past.

Sales of ski equipment include skis, ski poles and ski bindings and most of these are imported from France, Germany and Italy. For these European manufacturers, worldwide sales of winter sports gear have slumped considerably over the last five years, and the large ski manufacturers like Rossignol and Salomon have trimmed manufacturing costs and laid off large numbers of workers. Even though snow cover has been adequate in the USA and Japan and ski sales have held up there, the strength of European currencies against the dollar and the yen presented European manu-facturers, who rely heavily on exports to these two markets, with a foreign exchange problem (see Table 2.9). In the UK the market for skis has fallen dramatically – 71 per cent between 1988–9 and 1993–4 (see Table 2.10). An estimated 13,500 pairs of skis and 8,500 snowboards were sold in the season 1994–5 (Balmer 1995). Sales of boots in the UK rose to a peak in the 1988–9 season, mainly caused by a change from traditional front-clipped boots to new 'rear-entry' boots. However, since then the

Table 2.8 Sales of skiing goods, 1990–1 and 1993–4. *Source*: Mintel (1994).

| | 1990–1 | | 1993–4 | | % change |
	£m	%	£m	%	1990–4
Ski clothing	47.5	62	34.0	63	–28.4
Ski equipment	7.0	9	4.9	9	–30.0
Ski boots	7.7	10	5.6	10	–27.3
Accessories	13.9	18	9.6	18	–30.9
Total	76.1	100	54.1	100	–28.9

Table 2.9 World market for downhill skis, 1989. *Source*: Fraser (1990).

| | Volume | Value |
	%	
Japan	24.1	29.0
USA	21.3	21.1
Germany	12.4	10.5
Switzerland	8.1	7.7
France	7.5	6.1
Italy	6.5	6.6
Canada	6.1	5.5
Austria	4.2	4.0
Other countries	9.8	9.6

Table 2.10 Sales of ski equipment, 1988/9 to 1993/4. *Source*: Mintel (1994).

	£ m	Index	% change
1988–9	17.0	100	
1989–90	14.0	82	–18
1990–1	7.0	41	–50
1991–2	6.8	40	–3
1992–3	5.7	34	–16
1993–4 (estimate)	4.9	29	–14

Table 2.11 Sales of ski boots in the UK, 1988/9 to 1993/4. *Source*: Mintel (1994).

	£ m	Index	% change
1988–9	9.2	100	
1989–90	9.0	98	–2
1990–1	7.7	84	–14
1991–2	6.9	75	–10
1992–3	6.5	71	–6
1993–4	5.6	61	–14

market has slumped: Table 2.11 shows that sales of ski boots fell by nearly 40 per cent in five years. The big trend in ski boot design in recent years has been away from the rear-entry models that accounted for 80 per cent of all sales in the late 1980s, and back to conventional three or four clip front-entry overlap-shell models.

In the past, major companies in the industry kept within their own business, but recently the market has become much more competitive. Salomon, traditionally a boot and binding maker, entered the ski market in 1990 with the launch of a prestigious new racing ski. Rossignol, who had always concentrated on making skis, recently bought the Italian ski boot maker Lange, and soon after launched a Rossignol boot.

Sales of ski clothing have been equally disastrous. The sector had enjoyed strong growth rates through the 1980s, as ski anoraks became fashionable street-wear. This trend has now faded and the market plunged by 55 per cent between 1989 and 1994 (see Table 2.12). The major manufacturer for ski clothing in the UK is the department store C&A, which sells around 35 per cent of all clothing under its Rodeo brand. The top-selling independent brand is Nevica, with about 15 per cent of the market. Other brands with much smaller shares include Campari, Lutha, Berghaus, Killy and Head (Mintel 1994). All manufacturers in this market have suffered declining sales over the last decade. Owing to the mild winters of the early 1990s, skiers had little need for heavy anoraks and windscheaters. Rossignol even disposed of its clothes subsidiaries Anoralp and Veleda (which sells under the Killy brand name), and is concentrating instead on high-margin accessories like gloves, ski bags, sweatshirts and rucksacks. Other manufacturers are relying on the booming snowboarding market for their business. The owners of many Alpine ski shops now know that snowboarders account for anything up to 30 per cent of their winter business. In addition, most of the real fashion innovations are coming from companies such as Oxbow and Quicksilver that design clothes primarily for boarders rather than skiers. Sales of snowboards are running at around 10,000 a year, and an average expenditure of £350–£400 on boards and bindings would mean that the equipment market for snowboarding is worth around £4 million. Skis, too, are increasingly influenced by the snowboard culture in terms of cosmetic design and graphics. The revolutionary Atomic Powder Plus ('Fat Boys') owes its origins to the snowboard: it was invented by an Austrian engine driver who had studied the way boards cut through the snow. A narrower form of powder ski, the Explosiv, was introduced by Volkl a few years ago in response to the need for a ski that provided an acceptable compromise between deep snow stability and all-round versatility. According to some ski writers, the Fat Boys have brought powder skiing within the reach of most intermediate skiers, and the Americans believe they will have a big influence on the regeneration of their ski business (Heard 1996).

Table 2.12 Sales of ski clothing in the UK, 1988/9 to 1993/4. *Source*: Mintel (1994).

	£ m	Index	% change
1988–9	75	100	
1989–90	65	87	–13
1990–1	48	64	–26
1991–2	44	59	–8
1992–3	40	53	–9
1993–4 (estimate)	34	45	–15

In a mature market, the big manufacturers like Rossignol and Salomon are having to place more emphasis on technical innovation and competition to improve their profit margins. In addition to spreading their activities across all sectors of the ski market, most manufacturers are attempting to reduce their dependence on skiing by entering less weather-sensitive sports like golf and tennis. Rossignol have experienced limited success from their diversification into the manufacture of tennis rackets, and Salomon have fared only a little better from their move into making golf-clubs. With winter sports under a cloud and no bright light appearing from summer alternatives, some analysts are predicting that there will have to be further concentration in the equipment and clothing sectors (Fraser 1990).

CONCLUSION

The current ski market is estimated at some 65–70 million skiers worldwide, with the USA and Japan generating about 20 million of these. The skiing market is mature in Europe, as well as in Japan and North America, and will evolve more quickly in areas such as eastern Europe, Korea and southeast Asia. The total market in the UK consists of nearly 4 million people who have skied in the last five years. In 1997, approximately 700,000 skiing holidays were sold in the United Kingdom.

Skiing in the USA is concentrated in a few main areas, and differs from European skiing in many ways. Canada, like the USA, has recently been very successful in attracting European and Japanese skiers. The major ski areas of Europe – France, Italy, Austria, Switzerland and Germany – have suffered as a result. Sales of ski clothing and equipment also witnessed dramatic falls in the 1990s as they are reliant largely on the fortunes of the skiing holiday market. This has forced many ski manufacturers to diversify into the manufacture of alternative sports equipment such as tennis and golf. Sales of snowboarding equipment, however, have been quite buoyant and now account for as much as 30 per cent of toal sales. Snowboarding fashions have also had a major influence on the design of ski clothing and equipment.

CASE STUDY: VERBIER, SWITZERLAND

Verbier, at a height of 5000 feet, lies in the heart of the Swiss Alps, near the Italian border and the famous Grand St Bernard 'hospice', well-known for its rescue dogs. It is at the centre of one of the largest skiing areas in the world, the Four Valleys, which boasts over 400 km of ski-runs and 100 lifts. The skiing area of the Four Valleys connects the ski-runs of Verbier, La Tzoumaz, Nendaz, Veysonnaz and Val de Bagnes/Entremont. Verbier is Switzerland's best resort for range and ruggedness of skiing, and is well-known for its off-piste skiing.

A short history of Verbier is given on page 44. It has grown dramatically since the first skiers arrived at the beginning of the century. Figure 2.1 shows Verbier in 1933 and then in the 1970s. Made up of chalet-style houses, giving it the atmosphere of a large village, Verbier has 15,000 beds divided between hotels, chalets and apartments. Since 1980 yearly overnight stays have remained pretty stable at about one million. It is now both a winter and summer resort, and offers a wide range of sports and cultural activities. Verbier lies 435 miles from Paris, 168 miles from Milan, and 160 miles from Geneva and its international airport. It is just 30 miles from the Valais highway. It caters for visitors from all over the world, although 50 per cent of them are Swiss.

Figure 2.1 Verbier's growth between 1933 and the 1970s.

HISTORY OF VERBIER

1910   The first skiers arrive in the Val de Bagnes. Verbier is still a mainly summer pasture for cattle, including a few *mayens* (typical small wooden houses). *La Maison des Chanoines*, with the addition of a few guest rooms, accommodates the rare foreign visitors to the valley.

1925   The first skiers appear on the slopes of Verbier. They walk up from Sembrancher, 15 km lower down in the valley.

1927   Paul Fellay and Marcel Michellod give their first ski lessons as Verbier sees the opening of its first hotel.

1933   The Verbier Swiss Ski School is founded with Michellod as the first director.

1937   The Development Society of Verbier is founded, its main objectives being 'to develop the resort stimulating the touristic infrastructure, attracting new guests, and taking all useful measures to make the tourists' stay as pleasant as possible'.

1945   Dr Meili, from the Federal Office of Transport, publishes a report in order to ensure that Verbier will not plunge into uncontrolled development. It suggests a maximum of 2500 beds. At this time only 27 people live in Verbier all year round.

1946   The 'Funiluge', the ancestor of our modern lifts, is opened. A combustion engine, that has to be started by hand, activates a cable to which is fixed a giant sledge with room for twelve people. The cable is attached to a tree and pulls the sledge up for 200 metres. The following year Verbier's first serious ski-lift is built, with a total length of 250 metres.

1950   Five members of the Development Society decide to link Verbier up to the Croix-des-Ruinettes by cable. *The Télésiège de Medran s.a.* company is created with Rudolph Tissières, a lawyer from Martigny, as its director. The chair-lift is inaugurated in December, and the effect is immediate, with skiers arriving in massive numbers.

1957   The Attelas cable-car is constructed.

1961   The Mont Gele and Tortin cable-cars are constructed.

1962   Verbier has its own church and local priest.

1965   Fifteen years after the opening of the first chair-lift, Verbier's lift system is capable of carrying more than 10,000 people an hour. The total tourist turnover represents 25 million Swiss francs.

1975   The Chable-Verbier cable-car is built.

1983   The Tortin–Gentianes–Mont Fort cable-cars are opened.

1987   Diana Ross opens the 'Jumbo', linking La Chaux to the Col des Gentianes. The Jumbo is at this point Switzerland's largest cable-car, with a capacity of 150 people every six minutes.

1994   The 'Funispace' is built at a cost of 27 million Swiss francs. It links Les Ruinettes to Les Attelas.

1998   The new Tortin–Col de Chassoure cable-car is installed. It has eight-seater cabins with an initial uplift of 1200 persons per hour, extendable to 1600 persons per hour.

Figure 2.2 The first télésiège in Verbier and the new funitel.

The company responsible for Verbier's skiing, and arguably the most powerful stakeholder in the resort, is Téléverbier. Téléverbier started its life under the name of the Télésiège de Medran in 1950, and changed to Téléverbier in 1966. The company claims that its number one objective is to continue progress by replacing obsolete equipment with the most up-to-date technology, while ensuring comfort and operational efficiency. Téléverbier is a limited company with capital of 15 million francs, divided into 40,000 bearer shares. The annual turnover is between 34 and 37 million francs, with an average cash flow of approximately 10 million. Total investment to date has been 215 million francs.

Of the 43 lifts, there are four cable-cars, one *funitel* (baptised the 'Funispace' by staff), seven gondolas, nineteen chair-lifts, and twelve ski-tows. The lift with the greatest performance is the *funitel* which can carry 2000 people every hour. Invented by a French engineer, this ultra-modern system was developed and patented in Switzerland by the firm of Garaventa in Goldau, canton of Schwytz. Téléverbier was the first to construct a funitel in Switzerland. Figure 2.2 shows the contrast between the first télésiège in Verbier, the télésiège de Medran, and the new funitel.

Téléverbier employs about 100 staff during the year to operate its 43 lifts, and this figure rises to 345 during the ski season. The cost is around 15 million francs per year. Téléverbier offers its clients some 200 km of pistes which include lifts in Verbier, La Tzoumaz, Nendaz, Veysonnaz and Thyon. The total uplift capacity is 42,000 people an hour; on some weekends 120,000–130,000 trips are recorded, making up a total of some 12 million for the whole winter season. Téléverbier estimates that 700,000 lift passes are issued each year. Although the lift pass is one of the most expensive in Europe, Téléverbier has made an effort in the last few years to offer value for money. Prices were actually reduced in the 1996–7 season, and they remained stable for the winter of 1997–8. There is a very competitive family rate – up to 30 per cent reduction – and a 15 per cent discount for those aged between seventeen and twenty has recently been introduced.

The company has invested quite heavily over the last few years in upgrading its facilities because of the recession of the early 1990s; increased competition; and customer complaints about the poor service quality provided by Téléverbier (see Hudson and Shepherd, 1998). Verbier has always suffered from a reputation for long queues, and one of the major culprits has been the bottle-neck at the bottom of the Tortin–Chassoure lift. This lift (which was 25 years old) has just been replaced by a new cable-car, and this has had a dramatic effect on the queues. Passengers ride the 700 m height difference and 2.2 km distance in just 6 minutes 20 seconds. The installation was built by Caraventa, and cost about 11 million Swiss francs. Téléverbier has also just introduced a new ticket system – 'sport access' –

Figure 2.3 Paragliding in Verbier.

at all main, as well as at certain other strategic, points of access to the lift system. Ski passes of more than three days are printed on a smartcard that contains client information together with a photo of the user. The card, the size of a credit card, allows hands-off access to all lifts where electronic control units are installed. Monitor screens showing the photo of the pass holder provides verification of a match between card and user.

Snow-making facilities have also improved over the last decade, and Téléverbier says that 12 km of runs are equipped with snow-making machinery. A further improvement is the installation of loudspeakers at the main lift stations that provide advice for customers during the day on weather and snow conditions. Details of snow conditions are also updated every day on the Internet, and these same web pages provide live information on high latitude conditions via a camera located on the Attelas (at 2720 m).

In past years, the resort of Verbier has attracted many high-profile events, including the Swiss Championships, the Swiss Carving Cup, Alpine Ski World Cups, World Paragliding Championships and the Swiss Mountain Bike Championships. One event that has received particular attention from the media is the Verbier Xtreme Freeride Contest. Launched for the first time in 1996, this competition has already become the world's most widely reported international snowboard contest.

The competition is a unique spectacle. It is open by invitation only to the world's best boarders who compete at Bec des Rosses, opposite the Col des Gentianes. The mountain itself is at an altitude of 3222 m, and has gradients of between 45 and 55 degrees. The contestants climb to the top on foot, wearing a helmet, shoulder harness, back protector, avalanche victim detector, rucksack, shovel and probe. The entire event is held under the supervision of guides posted on the rock-face; doctors are ready to intervene; and a helicopter with full medical equipment is on standby a few hundred metres away. The organizers claim that the main goal is to put across an accident prevention message and to warn against the risks of off-piste snowboarding (which are too often disregarded by young devotees of powder snow). In a way that was probably not intended, this message has been transmitted. In 1998 a horrific fall in the women's event led to its cancellation, and a heavy fall in the men's event held up proceedings for about an hour. Nonetheless, several thousand spectators filled the square in Verbier to watch the prize-giving, and the event was shown on television that very evening.

Like many Alpine resorts, Verbier has invested heavily in developing all-year-round attractions. It offers over 400 km of hiking paths, with the opportunity to take photographs of chamois, ibex and marmots, and to admire various species of orchids and rhododendrons. Mountain biking is a very popular activity during the summer, as is golf (there is an eighteen-hole course located at the top of the village). Verbier is also said to be the 'mecca of paragliding', because of the exceptional flying sites (Figure 2.3 shows a paraglider in Verbier). The sports centre is open throughout the year and contains an indoor and outdoor swimming pool, an indoor ice-rink, curling, tennis, squash, sauna and solarium. Verbier has also made an effort to attract the conference and incentive market. The *Hameau de Verbier* includes a large 300-seat conference room, plus several smaller conference venues. The *hameau* (hamlet) also includes a restaurant, shops and a museum, all built around a village square with its own chapel recreating the atmosphere of a Valaisan hamlet. In 1994 the 'Verbier Festival and Academy' was introduced, and it has proved very popular in the summer months. The festival usually includes over 40 concerts, performances and workshops in music, theatre and dance. In addition to inviting some of the world's most celebrated musicians, the priority of the festival is to develop the talent of young artists. The 'open door' policy of the festival allows the public to freely attend the master classes, orchestra rehearsals, conferences and improvised performances.

CHAPTER 3

Distribution of the Skiing Product

INTRODUCTION

The channels of distribution used to attract customers to the slopes are a critical element in the study of the ski industry. Increasingly, changes in the structure of the industry and in technology have required organizations to reassess their distribution strategies. This chapter takes a closer look at the strategies employed on both sides of the Atlantic. Destinations in North America have traditionally sought to market their products and services directly to skiers, whereas destinations in Europe have relied on tour operators to bring British skiers to the slopes. This chapter focuses on the operations of such tour operators, using Crystal Holidays as a case study.

3.1 DISTRIBUTION CHANNELS IN THE UK

A number of different purchase channels are available to skiers in the UK. In addition to retail travel agents, ski holidays can be booked directly through the tour operators, or do-it-yourself packages can be assembled by making arrangements directly with accommodation suppliers in the resort. The distribution channel used varies according to a number of factors, including skill level, destination and income (Richards 1995). In general, the less experienced the skier, the more likely he or she is to use retail travel agents (see Table 3.1). This is because booking direct with tour operators or resort-based suppliers generally requires more product knowledge on the part of the consumer than using a travel agent. Despite the fact that 60–65 per cent of all skiing holidays are booked through a travel agent (Mintel 1996), the growing vertical integration in the travel trade has made it increasingly difficult for smaller operators to get good racking space in the larger multiples and this has led to more direct selling. Tour operators that deal directly with the public tend to be smaller, specialist companies that sell only skiing holidays. Although these companies save the cost of the travel agency commission, they tend to sell more exclusive, up-market holidays than the larger companies, and the average holiday price is therefore higher. The exception to this pattern is found in companies selling ski holidays to school parties or large groups: they also often sell direct, but in the form of low-priced group tours (Richards 1995).

Table 3.1 Distribution channel used by level of skier. *Source*: Richards (1995).

Mode of holiday purchase	Respondents (%)		
	Advanced	Intermediate	Beginner
Travel agent	41	51	66
Direct from tour operator	33	29	17
Made own travel arrangements	26	20	17
Total	100	100	100

The brochure is still the most powerful marketing tool for the large operators. For example, the 1997–8 Crystal Holidays ski brochure was 388 pages, with prices leading in at £175 for one week's self-catering in the Pyrenees. Traditionally, brochures came out in early summer, but operators are increasingly producing preview brochures in order to encourage skiers to book early. Some operators have tried dedicated snowboarding brochures, but these have been unsuccessful. For example, the Inghams programme, called *The Edge*, has been dropped for 1997–8 and incorporated into the core brochure in order to increase its racking. Other operators are using new technologies to distribute their product. Virgin Holidays have started selling the first-ever 'Ski-D Rom', claiming it to be Britain's first interactive ski holiday brochure ('Virgin's high-tech "brochure" triumph' 1996). The disc is a techno-guide to ski holidays in California, New England and Utah, as featured by the tour operator. The disc includes videos of resort areas, 'virtual' helicopter tours of three of them, interactive ski trail maps, as well as a variety of puzzles and games.

The trend towards late booking could benefit the travel agent, but an increasing number of bookings are made via teletext, and it will not be long before skiing holidays are being sold through the Internet. Richards (1995), in his survey of 100 UK travel agents, found that an appreciable information gap exists between retail travel agents and potential ski-product purchasers. This information deficiency on the part of the retailer leads to experienced skiers finding alternative purchase channels for ski products. As experienced skiers also tend to be those with higher incomes and levels of ski-holiday consumption, the resulting loss of potential revenue to agents is likely to be much greater.

Richards believes that while it may be difficult for travel agents to meet the information needs of an increasingly demanding clientele, there is room for 'no-frills' products, even at the top end of the market. The major growth area in the European tour-operating industry is 'part packages' – individual holiday elements, such as airline seats or hotel beds, that allow the tourist to assemble his or her own holiday. The current research indicates that a high proportion of skilled consumers are assembling their own ski holidays, using their own extensive product knowledge. For those on high incomes, creating such holidays can involve high opportunity costs compared with buying a package through a travel agent. If agents can learn to use the new potential of Computer Reservation Systems (CRS) and the Internet, they can tap a lucrative new market.

3.2 DISTRIBUTION CHANNELS IN NORTH AMERICA

Destinations in North America have traditionally sought to market their products and services directly to skiers. However, as the range of on-site facilities and services has expanded, and as the competition for markets has increased, so has the need to develop indirect linkages with skiers through distribution intermediaries. These distribution channels are most frequently developed in ski areas where there is a significant physical distance between the producer and the consumer, or where there is a considerable investment in on-site facility capacity requiring high levels of use in order to retain viability. Williams and Dossa (1998) have plotted the distribution of direct and indirect channel use by British Columbia's skiers (see Table 3.2). As British Columbia's ski industry has grown in both capacity and services, its need for a wide variety of product distribution channels has expanded dramatically. Travel agents and airline intermediaries operate a distribution channel of growing significance (nearly 12 per cent of respondents), while club channelers provide a second form of product distribution for the British Columbia winter resort industry (approximately 10 per cent). Club channelers are frequently ski club managers who are primarily interested in facilitating ski travel for their members. They act as reference groups for many skiers and serve to increase the diffusion of information about alternative ski destinations (Rand 1995). A third distribution channel comprises on-site destination marketing organizations. Channel intermediaries in this group include ski area sales personnel and other on-site destination marketing organizations. About 29 per cent of all visitors in the study indicated that they use this more direct distribution channel to arrange their accommodation. A final ski channel identified by Williams and Dossa was the direct channel. Visitors using direct channels arranged their accommodation directly with lodging suppliers, in the process bypassing many potential intermediaries. Accommodation arrangements were confirmed either prior to arrival or upon visiting the destination. About 49 per cent of all visitors fell into this category.

Table 3.2 Distribution of respondents by channel type. *Source*: Williams and Dossa (1998).

Channel intermediaries used	Respondents (%)
Indirect	
Travel agent	10.6
Airline	0.9
Ski club	3.7
Organized club	6.3
Total indirect	21.5
Direct	
Resort association	11.9
Accommodations	17.1
No arrangements made	49.4
Total direct	78.5

As can be seen from Table 3.2, about 78 per cent of all respondents interviewed were direct, and 22 per cent were indirect, channel users. So there are significant differences between the North American and UK skiing market in terms of distribution. While the two groups visiting British Columbia were similar in many ways, several socio-demographic, trip planning, and travel behaviour factors distinguished them. As a group, direct channel users were much more impulsive and family focused in their ski travel planning and trip behaviour. On average they were significantly older and better educated than their indirect channel counterparts (similar to their counterparts in the UK). They were also significantly more likely to spend less time planning their ski vacations in advance, more often depending on information gleaned from less formal sources of information (e.g. friends and family) to make trip decisions. Indirect channel users, in contrast, tended to be more cautious and formal in their trip decision-making. They were significantly more likely to be younger, single and less educated than their direct channel counterparts, and their visits to ski destinations tended to be longer. Unlike British skiers, there were no significant differences in skill levels between the two groups. Williams and

Dossa suggest that in order to develop truly effective marketing strategies, destination marketers should acquire information concerning the characteristics of different types of channel users. To acquire such information, existing and potential markets could be segmented on the basis of the channels of distribution they use. Such market intelligence can be especially useful in determining which channels produce the largest number of visitors, greatest frequency of repeat business, longest periods of stay, and the best yield for the ski destination.

In North America and more recently Europe, many destinations are creating their own home pages on the Internet. Steamboat, Colorado, for example, has a website with over 200 pages of information and pictures of the resort (Nelson 1997). Conversions from Internet to sales are done on the phone where the resort acquires the credit card information. To save paperwork and aid in making reservations, Steamboat has developed a 'Book-it' form that guests fill out and send by e-mail. At Vail resorts the number of Internet requests for information now far exceeds inquiries from other sources. Vail properties received over 40,000 inquiries through the Web during the 1997–8 season; this led to the booking of 4650 room nights – a conversion rate of 19 per cent (Castle 1998). (This was roughly equivalent to the conversion rate achieved through the travel trade (20.6 per cent) and fulfilment programmes (21.4 per cent).)

In fact, many resorts in the USA are finding that the Internet is working well for them. Data from the 1997–8 NSAA National Skier/Snowboarder Demographic Study illustrate the demographic similarities between skiers and Internet users generally, while also showing high levels of Internet access among most sub-segments of the skier/snowboarder population (Rosall 1998). Internet access is somewhat higher among US skiers than among international visitors to the United States; rapid growth in Internet usage is, however, occurring overseas, especially among the younger, more affluent, educated consumers. Rosall found that for many resorts, the venture online has been highly cost-effective, with a far lower cost impression than for other media and a much more targeted audience. Additionally, the Internet is providing new and powerful ways for resorts and consumers to communicate. As technology advances and Internet usage expands, the power and versatility of the Internet as a marketing and communications tool is sure to grow.

With all the advances in website graphics and design, it is interesting to note that conventional marketing materials such as brochures are still in great demand in North America. Indeed, some resorts are having to increase their brochure print-runs in order to keep up with requests from their website visitors. The pattern illustrates that for all the improvements in website technology, it has a long way to go before making more traditional media obsolete – if it ever does.

3.3 SKIING TOUR OPERATORS

Tour operating

In tour operating in general, the trend in the past few years is for the few big travel companies to acquire many of the smaller ones. Thomson, Britain's biggest tour operator, started it all in 1998 by spending £10 million buying Ausbound and Austravel; Airtours then bought up Cresta and Bridge Travel Group. In June, Thomas Cook, which already owns Sunworld, paid £65 million for another tour operator, Flying Colours. That summer saw a buying frenzy: First Choice bought Unijet and Hayes and Jarvis; Airtours spent £80 million buying Direct Holidays; and Thomson made a purchase that could have a significant impact on the future of the skiing market – the buying of Crystal. The result is that the biggest four tour operators in the UK now control about 75 per cent of the overseas package holiday market. The first three, Thomson, Airtours and Thomas Cook, also own the top three travel agencies – Lunn Poly, Going Places and Thomas Cook respectively – and these openly promote their in-house holidays.

Ski operators

One subject guaranteed to spark off a lively debate among ski tour operators is the overall size, and their respective share, of the ski market. When launching its industry overview in 1997, Crystal Holidays sought to improve on Stats M. R. and Mintel figures by including the smaller operators and the independent sector. They divided the market into three sectors: tour operator business, which generated sales of 475,000 in the 1996–7 season; independent skiers at around 205,000; and schools at 150,000. The report (Crystal Holidays 1997) also shows (perhaps not surprisingly) Crystal as the clear market leader with a 23.7 per cent market share (see Table 3.3). However, the acquisition of Crystal in August 1998 thrust Thomson into pole position as number one operator in the ski market, nearly double the size of its nearest rivals. According to figures from industry statistics firm A. C. Neilsen, the combined carryings of the two operators in the winter 1997–8 period to April was 131,895 – a 37.3 per cent share of the total UK market. This is based on Crystal's ski carryings of 80,637 last winter (a market share of 22.8 per cent), against Thomson's 51,258 (a 14.5 per cent share). The figures exclude direct sales and schools' business that boost Thomson's joint operations closer to 200,000. The move places Inghams firmly in the number two spot. Last winter's figures showed the operator had 19.9 per cent of the market with 70,000 carryings, although Inghams claimed bookings of 108,000.

It is clear from statistics that independent and direct bookings have increased at a much faster rate than tour operator bookings through travel agents. It is estimated that around 70 per cent of the market books through an operator and 30 per cent travels independently (Mintel 1996). To support the growing independent market for skiing holidays, the ferry companies have launched all-inclusive, ski–drive packages; the channel tunnel has also provided a boost to the self-drive independent market. Continued improvements to the European motorway network now allow easy travel to within the last few miles of major resorts in France, Switzerland and Austria. The channel tunnel has increased the popularity of snow-trains, and the coach market is now virtually non-existent.

Table 3.3 Total tour operator market 1996–7. *Source*: Crystal Holidays (1997).

Operator	Passengers	Market share (%)
Crystal	112 500	23.7
Inghams	95 000	20.0
First Choice	77 000	16.2
Thomson	56 500	11.9
Nielson	39 500	8.3
Airtours	34 000	7.1
Others	60 500	12.8

It is not just the growing trend in independent bookings that has affected the industry's 200 tour operators. Since the start of the 1990s they have had to deal with the impact of the recession on skiing holidays; poor weather conditions adding to the trend towards later booking; and the devaluation of sterling, which has forced operators to increase prices. In an attempt to stimulate demand, tour operators have introduced snow guarantees, new destinations, early booking incentives and more flights from regional airports. However, these moves increased their costs and had only a limited effect on stimulating the market. The result was heavy discounting and the production of second and even third brochures with reduced rates. Consequently, margins and profitability have been extremely low (Mintel 1994). However, sales for the 1997–8 season were much improved, and the choice of both ski and snowboard holidays was wider than ever in the 1998–9 season (with 28 bonded tour operators promoting 270 resorts in 18 countries).

Operators can be categorized according to destination: the mainstream carriers like Crystal and Thomson who go everywhere; smaller firms like Mark Warner and Club Med that have resorts in several countries; those such as Meriski and Ski Verbier who specialize in one country or region; those such as as Finlays and Peak

Figure 3.1 Some specialist holidays include race training.

Ski who specialize in one or two resorts; and the 'boutique' operators that focus on a single market. Small firms specializing in everything from children, to cross-country, to Christian holidays continue to challenge the mainstream operators. The ski business resembles the long-haul market in that while it is well served by the major operators, there is still room, and a need, for some highly specialized companies. Winter sports specialists cover a range of products, from single destinations and small chalet accommodation, to catering for the skills aspect of skiing. (The latter can include tuition in powder skiing, race training (see Figure 3.1) and bump skiing.) Most of these companies make no pretence of the high cost of their holidays.

Goodall and Bergsma (1993), made a comparison between skiing holidays offered by UK and Dutch mass-market tour operators in order to illustrate the similarities and contrasts in tour operators' strategies in developing their package holiday portfolios. They saw a trend towards the concentration of skiing opportunities in mass-market tour operator programmes which went hand in hand with the standardization of the product. They also found that the distinctions between mass-market tour operators rest not so much on the range of resorts and their skiing and non-skiing characteristics, as on the brochure images conveying the 'product brand' and on the prices asked.

It is difficult to calculate the proportion of operators' advertising spent on skiing products, because the published data refers to an overall holiday advertising spend. Skiing holiday advertising, however, can be found in the quality Sunday newspapers from around November through to March. The *Sunday Times* claims to attract 345,000 of the estimated 1.5 million British skiers, compared with 250,000 who read the *Mail on Sunday* and 211,000 who read the Daily Telegraph. (These figures are based on the twelve months to September 1995 (Mintel 1996)) The sport is also widely covered by the media. The BBC's *Ski Sunday* has been running for almost twenty years and averages 3 million viewers, despite growing competition from *Eurosport*. The spectacular mountain scenery and the occasional crash attract the audience, and the theme tune – 'Pop Looks Bach' by Fontaine – is widely thought to be the most stirring in televised sport. The programme does not try to blind viewers with ski science, and former presenter David Vine has never skied.

Specialist magazines also cover skiing, the most popular of these being the the *Good Ski Guide*, *Ski and Snowboard*, the *Daily Mail Ski Magazine* and *Ski Special*. Furthermore, there are several annual ski exhibitions around the country, the biggest being the *Daily Mail* Ski Show at Olympia in London.

Resort operations for tour operators

Tour operators rely to a great extent on temporary employees for overseas operations during the winter. For the larger tour operators, recruitment for overseas employment begins in June and continues until the end of October. Those working in Europe have to be available from the end of November until the middle of April, whereas North American staff must be away from mid-November to the end of April. Owing to work permit restrictions, preference is given to EC passport holders for work in Europe, and to USA/Canada nationals for work in their home countries. Some of the key jobs are resort representatives, chalet representatives/catering staff, hotel staff, ski guides and nannies.

Resort representatives are responsible for all aspects of the smooth running of a resort. Relevant experience in a customer service environment is usually required and representatives should be capable of working on their own initiative. They work on their own or as part of a team, depending on the size of operations in the resort. The 'reps' are usually responsible for the transfer to and from the resort; the ordering of lift passes for the clients; the booking of equipment hire and ski-school classes; and the organizing of any non-ski activities in the resort. They would also have to deal with problems in the resort such as accidents, staff problems or maintenance problems.

The chalet representatives are responsible for the smooth running of the chalets in the resort, and the job involves day-to-day contact with the guests. Duties include preparing breakfast, afternoon tea with home-baked cakes, and a three-course dinner with wine. With chalets of more than twelve guests, companies usually employ couples or friends, but one person is expected to look after six to twelve skiers without additional assistance. Operators do not always insist on written qualifications, but some catering experience is essential for these demanding jobs. For the larger chalets and hotels, experienced chefs are recruited who are assisted by waitresses and chambermaids. Hotel managers are employed to oversee the running of the larger, operator-owned hotels.

One ingredient that most operators like to offer their clients is the free use of ski guides in the resort. However, ski resorts in many European countries are making it very difficult for the operators to offer this service. In many Swiss resorts, tour operators are allowed to offer guiding for only one or two days a week. In France the situation is more controversial, with many UK guides threatened with violence and arrest. The Association of British Tourists (ABTA) is lobbying the European Commission over this long-running dispute. The Association is seeking to clarify regulations that require already qualified UK instructors and guides to take French ski exams before they can work. These days it is the resort representatives who often double up as ski guides, in order to introduce the slopes to clients on the first couple of days of their holiday.

With the expansion of chalets, and the increase in the number of young families going to the Alps, the employment of nannies has become essential. Usually they are required to have a nannying or equivalent qualification, together with some practical experience. Children's representatives are also employed to look after older children; this often involves a pick-up/drop-off service for ski school, lunchtime supervision, and half-day organized activities in the morning or afternoon.

CONCLUSION

The marketing channels employed to bring skiers to destinations are a critical part of the marketing mix, and this chapter has highlighted the key differences between the distribution channels used in North America and Europe. The majority of British skiers still use brochures and book their holidays through tour operators, whereas in North America skiers tend to make direct reservations with their chosen destination. On both sides of the Atlantic the Internet is becoming increasingly powerful as a marketing tool for ski destinations.

CASE STUDY: CRYSTAL HOLIDAYS

Background

> With a tough two or three years coming to the holiday market place, he who controls distribution will control the business . . .
>
> (Travel analyst Michael East, commenting in *Travel Weekly* on the mania for takeovers infecting the high street in 1998; see East (1998, p. 6))

In 1996 the Monopolies and Mergers Commission (MMC) was asked to investigate the supply in the UK of travel agents' and tour operators' services in relation to foreign package holidays. The Director-General of Fair Trading (DGFT) had expressed concern about developments concerning vertically integrated groups. Independent participants in the travel trade, both tour operators and travel agents, argue that increasing vertical integration is bringing about various anti-competitive practices that will eventually squeeze them out of the market, leading to higher prices and less choice for the consumer. However, after two years of deliberations, the MMC report in 1998 argued that the anti-competitive effects of vertical integration are slight, and it did not condemn vertical integration as a whole in the travel trade.

One practice that was of some concern to the MMC was 'directional selling', which they define as the sale or attempted sale by a vertically integrated travel agent of the foreign package holidays of its linked tour operator in preference to the holidays of other tour operators. The practice is facilitated by the lack of transparency in ownership links. However, the MMC found no evidence that directional selling resulted in less value for money for consumers, and therefore did not find it to be against the public interest.

The MMC decision has only helped to fuel the buying frenzy in tour operating, and the massive consolidation of the UK tour operator sector has continued. It was only a matter of time before the agency sector followed suit. In just one week in the summer of 1998, nearly 2000 travel agency outlets within Thomas Cook and Carlson ownership, or within ARTAC or Advantage membership, either changed, or agreed to consider changing, their ownership or their business partner. That is nearly 30 per cent of all high-street agents. If one adds to that another 15 per cent of other independents that will be part of the 'Thomson Preferred Agents' and 'Airtours Partnership in Profit' schemes, and then mix in the 1500 or so agency outlets owned by Lunn Poly and Going Places, all of a sudden more than 4000 retail outlets – over 60 per cent of the total – could be either owned by, or contractually tied into preferring, one of the three major, vertically integrated companies. This group of multiples and high-producing independents accounts for an estimated 75 per cent of the business. The consolidation has not yet ended. Lunn Poly and Going Places are reportedly looking to expand their chains by as many as 500 outlets between them. In addition, First Choice has announced that it is going to build a network of more than 700 shops with a £60 million three-year investment, admitting that if it is to stay in the game, it needs tied distribution. First Choice had been the only one of the large travel companies without a travel agency chain. Ian Clubb, chairman of First Choice, said that it was a defensive reaction to what is happening in the industry, but First Choice's late entry into the travel agency marriage market has made it look like an ageing spinster desperately seeking a partner after all the eligible bachelors have been spoken for.

Crystal Holidays

We want to continue growing the business so we have to have a distribution channel that is fixed and safe.

(Crystal chief executive Peter Dyer justifying the sale of Crystal International Travel Group to Thomson for £66.2 m in August 1998; see Skidmore (1998, p. 1))

Crystal Holidays was formed in 1980 by Peter Dyer, managing director, and Darko Emersic, overseas director. Both had been in the travel business all their working lives, working with companies such as Clarksons, Lunn Poly, Swans and Inghams. Clive Brigham, operations director, joined the company in 1981, followed by Andy Appleton, commercial director, in 1983. Andy Perrin joined as the first Austrian resort representative in 1981, and, after managing the Austrian programme for eight years, returned to the UK to become the marketing director. More recent additions to the directors' team include David Rowe and Andrew Peters.

The company has seen incredible growth: operating in just three resorts in Austria in 1981, it now has a representation of 134 resorts in eleven countries worldwide. In 1997 it was the largest ski operator in the UK, offering the biggest programme and the largest chalet operation. Expanding the company's reputation as the leading specialist ski company has involved pioneering new programmes into the USA, Canada, Norway, plus tremendous expansion in Italy over the last decade. Crystal also provides services for corporate and incentive sales, which is a fast growing part of the ski market, headed by David Drake.

Crystal has also diversified its product offerings. The Lakes and Mountains programme has grown into an established leader in its field, as have Premier Britain, Premier Italy, Premier France, and Premier Cities. The Crystal Schools Programme offers both winter ski and summer activities for children. Crystal's full range of products can be seen in Table 3.4.

Table 3.4 Crystal products and specifications in 1998.

Crystal Ski	Jetsave
Crystal Lakes and Mountains	Jetsave Touring
Crystal Schools	Tropical Places – direct sell
Crystal Ireland	American Holidays
Crystal Premier Britain	Greyhound International
Crystal Premier Italy	Jersey and Guernsey Travel Service
Crystal Premier Cities	
Crystal Premier France	
Carryings	About 280,000 air packages and 100,000 land-based packages
Combined turnover	More than £200 m
Expected pre-tax profits	More then £3.4 m
Net assets	£13.2 m
Employees	330

Competition for Crystal in the ski market

Of the mainstream carriers, the principal competition for Crystal comes from Thomson, First Choice, Airtours and Inghams. First Choice Ski has its roots in the old Owners Abroad brands, Falcon and Enterprise. With an estimated share of 15–16 per cent, managing director Dermot Blastland claims First Choice is either number three in the market behind Crystal and Inghams or equal number two with Inghams. Having acquired Skibound in 1995 for £23 million, the operator ended 1997–8 with about 90,000 sales, but has a capacity of 101,000 holidays for 1998–9. Using partner Canada 3000's flights, First Choice is strong in Canada, but France still accounts for more than half of its programme. Thomson has increased its bookings by 45 per cent after a lengthy period of flat, if not falling, sales (Jones 1998). Airtours has entered the skiing market only in the last decade, and now accounts for about 7 per cent of holidays sold. It claims that North America accounts for 25 per cent of its total ski carryings. It has a dedicated charter-based brochure, and a brochure targeted at 18–35 year olds called *Escapade Ski*. Inghams is the UK arm of European tour operation Hotel Plan International, which is owned by Swiss-based conglomerate Migros. In 1996–7 it carried 95,000 passengers and commanded 20 per cent of the skiing market.

Recent events

In May 1991 Crystal acquired a new owner in the Dial Corporation of Phoenix, Arizona, a multi-billion dollar organization who bought the company for £4 m. Its enormous financial power allowed further expansion of the Crystal product range. In October 1997 a management buy-out to the tune of approximately £20 m saw chief executive Peter Dyer holding the reins again. Backed by investors Barclays Private Equity (BPE), who took 60 per cent of the ownership, Dyer created the Crystal International Travel Group.

The latest phase in the company's history came in August 1998, when Thomson beat off rivals Airtours and Kuoni to complete the £66.2 m acquisition of Crystal International Travel Group. City institutions such as BPE usually seek to pull out of companies after about three years, but this deal came only ten months after BPE's investment. Its managing director, Stephen Walton, said the Monopolies and Mergers Commission report in December 1998 had effectively given the go-ahead for big growth by major operators. This prompted a rash of takeovers and an early bidding war for Crystal.

Crystal will be part of Thomson's Breakaway division and the director will report to Lunn Poly managing director Ian Smith. Peter Dyer, who has now resigned from Crystal, said a key reason for the deal was distribution: 'We want to continue growing the business so we have to have a distribution channel that is fixed and safe.' Dyer (see Skidmore 1988) said the timing of the deal followed further consolidation of the industry: 'We did not want to be the only mid-sized operator . . . It is difficult to tell a bank that we should wait another two years before selling or floating considering the strength of the pound and buoyancy of the market.' Seventy Crystal employees shared a payout of £26.5 million following the Thomson deal.

Both ski brands will run independently for the time being, and Thomson have inserted a clause in the deal that will reduce the price by £10 m if Crystal's profits do not hit £3.4 m for the year to October 1998. Industry observers believe the £66 m price tag was too high for a company that was on course to make only £1.1 m for the year ending October 1997, prior to the management buy-out. Others have suggested that multiple agencies that have given strong support to Crystal may now not be so keen because it belongs to a major competitor in Lunn Poly. However, Thomson see Crystal's smaller specialist brands as big an attraction as the ski product. In addition it expects major synergies to be shared – by flying on Thomson-owned Britannia, and, in resort, on issues such as bed contracting.

The Crystal ski product will now receive greater exposure through Thomson-owned travel agent, Lunn Poly. This great increase in directional selling will be a critical factor for Crystal Holidays. Crystal has traditionally sold approximately 90 per cent of its holidays through travel agents and was anxious to ensure it had outlets for its products. Thomson claims that making Crystal part of a large group will lead to benefits that will be passed on to the public. However, critics suggest that the concentration of power in so few hands could lead to a reduction in choice and will enable the big companies to push up the price of holidays.

CHAPTER 4

The Consumer

INTRODUCTION

This chapter reviews the academic literature related to skiing and consumer behaviour. The research is not extensive, and there is considerable potential for expanding this body of research. The first section is an overview of general research into the skiing industry, including participation rates, demographics and consumption patterns of existing skiers. Previous research that supports marketing and product development programmes for skiing has focused primarily on gaining a better understanding of the socio-economic, attitudinal, and behavioural characteristics of existing skiers, and studies can be broadly categorized into those studies that look at the motivations of skiers and those that focus on destination choice.

The second part of this chapter contains a more detailed analysis of studies concerning the motivations of skiers. Various attempts have been made to segment the skiing market, and these are reviewed. The third section concentrates on the important, but under-researched, area of the non-skiing population, and the limited attempts by researchers to understand the constraints facing this segment of the population.

4.1 THE CONSUMER PROFILE

During the 1970s and early 1980s, skiing constituted one of the most popular and fastest growing outdoor recreation activities in the USA. One national study indicated that during 1980, there were approximately 14.6 million US skiers (Goeldner and Standley 1980). Another nationwide survey at that time identified 12.9 million Americans as active downhill skiers. Perhaps this popularity explains the proliferation of articles related to downhill skiing that came out of North America during the 1980s. According to the National Sporting Goods Association

Alpine skiers in the US are predominantly male (60 per cent), 35 years old and have a median household income of $56,614 a year. They are college educated and tend to have managerial or professional jobs. Besides skiing, they participate in tennis, cycling, sailing and racquetball, and are twice as likely to buy wine, invest in real estate and travel overseas as the average person. The majority of snowboarders are male (73 per cent), but snowboarding saw an 8 per cent point increase in women riders from 1995 to 1996. Snowboarders are young (more than 89 per cent are under 25), with the average age being 21. They live in a household that has a median income of $45,413. Many riders are students, and they like to mountain bike, hike, skateboard, surf and play video games.

According to the latest Mountain International Opinion Survey (MINOS) conducted in European ski resorts from December 1995 through April 1996, European skiing consumers are different from those in North America (Spring 1996b). Among European skiers, incomes tend to be lower, age is younger and self-ranked skier ability levels are lower. One significant difference is that European resorts draw a more cosmopolitan cast of skiers from around the world. They attract a greater number of Asians, South Americans and skiers from the Arabic countries, than do the United States resorts.

The MINOS study suggests that while resorts in the Alps generally offer more diverse activities to their winter visitors (nearly 15 per cent do not Alpine ski or snowboard) than do United States resorts, the remaining 85 per cent are most interested in snow cover. Snow (and sun) is what they come for. Terrain, so important to North American skiers, is less important to northern Europeans (except the Germans who tend to self-rank themselves as better skiers). The reasons have to do with the motivations to ski (vacation, relax, get-away, have a good time – as well as slide downhill) and the fact that most are intermediate skiers. Challenging terrain is of interest to southern Europeans, the countries that produce racers and Olympians. According to the survey, northerners tend to balance their downhill participation with a keen interest in basking in the sun, having a good lunch with a bottle of wine, and enjoying the conviviality of friends.

The MINOS study shows that the European skiers are taking ski holidays on average three out of every five seasons. The study distinguishes seven groups within the French population with regard to their consumption or non-consumption of winter sports over the previous five years. The seven groups are:

1. the *regulars*, representing 4.7 per cent of the French population aged over 14. This category (2.1 m people) constituted the main target group of the French ski resorts;

2. the *occasionals*, representing 7 per cent of the population (3.4 m people), who had stayed two or three times at ski resorts in the previous five years;

3. the *seldoms*, also representing 7 per cent of the population, who have stayed at a ski resort only once in the previous five years;
4. the *neighbours*, representing 10 per cent of the population, who spend very short periods at ski resorts and who live in the same area;
5. the *quitters*, 10 per cent of the population;
6. the *yet to be convinced*, representing 8 per cent of the population (3.5 m people), who are never involved in skiing activities but who claim they would be prepared to give it a try;
7. the *not to be convinced*, representing the majority of the French population (53 per cent), who have never been, and will probably never be, involved in skiing activities.

In spite of the relative lack of domestic skiing in the UK, the total ski market consists of about 7.5 million people who have skied at some time, of whom 3.75 million have skied in the past five years (Mintel 1994). Included in this total is a relatively small but important group of frequent, committed skiers. The Mintel report also indicates that the number of regular skiers grew by 5 per cent between 1985 and 1992, and, in addition, that ski club membership in the UK grew from 51,000 in 1983 to 71,000 in 1990 (Sports Council 1991). Mintel's latest survey (1996) went in some depth into frequency of skiing in order to isolate and profile the regular skier. They found that 2 per cent of adults had been skiing five times or more between 1990 and 1995. This is the core market of 1 million regular skiers, although the ski industry often uses a broader figure of 1.5 million active skiers as its yardstick. The 15–19 age group is twice as likely to be a regular skier reflecting the recent growth of the youthful snowboard market. In fact, British skiers are very youthful in comparison to the profile of skiers in most continental European nationalities. The statistics for UK skiers also show that 91 per cent of ABCs over 55 have never skied. Skiing is therefore a modern as well as a youthful and socio-economic group-related pastime.

In 1993 and 1996 the type of consumer who had ever skied was predominately male, aged between 15–34 years, and from the ABC socio-economic groups. Mintel believe that this confirms the notion that skiing is an up-market young man's sport, requiring a spirit of adventure, youth, energy and a degree of wealth. The type of adult of those ever having skied in 1989 was similar, but while numbers were equally matched between the sexes, the age profile was slightly younger and there was a higher proportion of skiers from the lower socio-economic groups. The Mintel figures suggest that in 1989 those choosing not to ski did so because they preferred to take an alternative form of holiday, while in 1993 the recession had hit those who still might have chosen a skiing holiday if they could afford one. It appears that by 1993 skiing had become much less of a mass-market activity, and this pattern has remained to this day. Only the most committed to the sport have continued to take skiing holidays.

Other surveys have attempted to understand the make-up of the British skier. A 1990 Sports Marketing survey (reported in Greer 1990) found that 63 per cent of skiers were in the ABC categories – professional, senior and junior management – and that skiers tended to be more sporty than the average individual, with 80 per cent playing at least one other sport on a regular basis. More men than women favoured skiing holidays in 1990, and they tended to be at a higher skiing standard than women. The average age of skiers was 29, with 80 per cent under 40. The survey also discovered that many skiers travel in groups, and it is the group leader who makes the choice of destination. If not in a group, the main criteria are the skier's previous experience of a resort and the price.

Precision Marketing ('Portrait of a skiing enthusiast' 1993) use data from N. D. L. Direct Marketing to build a profile of the skiing enthusiast. They say that most indicators point to skiers being affluent people, drawn from the professional and management classes. They cannot provide an accurate age profile, as the data is confused by the number of students and young people living at home who confess to taking part in skiing. However, lifestyle indicators were used to provide a fuller picture of how skiers spend their time when not skiing. The most outstanding pastime is sailing, closely followed by tennis and power-boating. Other strong links exist between skiing and interests in squash, cycling, and health and fitness. Aside from sporty activities, skiers are likely to be partial to theatre-going, good food and wines, and fine arts and antiques. They are also far more likely to be interested in stocks and shares or unit trusts than in bingo or doing the pools. *Precision Marketing* also reported that skiers are heavily represented in northern Scotland and south-east England.

The fact that skiing is a minority attraction to UK consumers means that the structure of the non-skiing population is just as illuminating as the skiing population. It is still the case that 97 per cent of the C2DEs aged over 55 have never experienced skiing. Among young, affluent consumers (ABC 15–34 year olds), the majority (61 per cent) have never skied, but a core enthusiastic group of ABC 15–34 year olds, 12 per cent of this group, had skied at least three times between 1990 and 1995.

The 1996 Mintel survey revealed that, regionally, London and the south had the highest proportion of both skiers and lapsed skiers, illustrating the depth of the recession in south-east England. Those least likely to ski were from the South-west/Wales and the North-west. These findings point to a core market whose propensity to be skiers is not only related to age but to a combination of socio-economic class and regional factors. This is elaborated in Table 4.1 with a break-down of skiing frequency.

The bias towards the pre-family stage among frequent skiers is basically a function of age in skiing, as in other sports, but the transition to family stage has resulted in the proportion of frequent skiers falling from 11 to 2 per cent as family commitments take hold. In many European countries where resorts are within driving distance, skiing has developed more as a family pursuit; however, in the UK the outbound market is still biased towards pre-family adults who can afford a skiing holiday. According to the data from Mintel, the arrival of family responsibilities and budgeting reduces the propensity to go skiing.

Consumer interest in skiing can be greatly stimulated by media coverage of skiing events, such as those held at the Winter Olympics. In addition, as suggested previously, the BBC's *Ski Sunday* has proved popular, as has specialist and national press coverage of the sport. Table 4.2 examines the demographic profile of those most interested in media coverage of the sport. Television is clearly the preferred medium as it lends itself more to the excitement and action-based nature of the sport. 16.6 per cent of consumers claimed to watch skiing on the television, compared to 1.9 per cent who claimed to read reports. Not surprisingly, those most interested in media coverage were those who participated in the sport: men, those in the 15–34 year-old age group, ABs and those in the higher household income brackets.

The notion of skilled consumption suggests that frequent participation in order to increase skill levels should be a prominent feature of activities such as skiing. Richards (1995), from a survey of 1415 UK skiers, discovered that advanced skiers take more skiing holidays than intermediate level skiers (see Table 4.3). Advanced skiers are almost twice as likely as intermediate skiers to take multiple ski holidays annually. Frequent participation in ski holidays by advanced skiers is also linked to a high overall level of holiday taking. The average advanced skier reported taking three long holidays (four or more nights) a year, compared with a mean of 2.5 holidays for intermediate skiers and 2.3 holidays a year for beginners. The duration of holiday taken is normally one week, although there has been an increase in specialist operators offering weekend breaks for skiers with more money than time. Swiss Travel Service recently reported that weekend ski breaks of three/four nights showed an 85 per cent increase year on year, while sales of holidays of 14 nights or more fell by 10 per cent (Lewis and Wild 1995).

Skiing is also making a come-back as an inspirational incentive for employees (O'Callaghan 1996). There are a number of specialist companies in the market, and even Crystal has recently launched a specialist incentive division to handle group business. The perceived value of such a trip is high, as skiing is still seen as an expensive sport that is out of most people's reach.

Table 4.1 Demographic details of regular skiers and non-skiers, 1995. *Source*: Mintel (1996).

Base: 2038 adults

		One or two times	Three or more times	Not in last five years	Never skied
				%	
All		6	5	5	83
Men		7	5	7	80
Women		5	4	4	87
	15–19	15	10	4	66
	20–24	10	6	4	66
	25–34	9	8	8	73
	35–44	4	3	8	83
	45–54	4	1	4	88
	55–64	4	2	2	93
	65+	1	*	3	95
AB		11	8	9	71
C1		8	7	6	80
C2		3	3	3	89
D		3	*	2	90
E		3	–	2	93
ABC	15–34	16	12	8	61
	35–54	7	5	8	79
	55+	2	2	4	91
C2DE	15–34	6	4	5	82
	35–54	2	1	4	92
	55+	1	–	2	97
London		7	5	7	78
South		4	5	10	81
Anglia/Midlands		7	3	5	84
South-west/Wales		4	3	3	87
Yorkshire/North East		4	3	4	89
North-west		6	4	4	85
Scotland		5	5	4	83
Pre-family		13	11	6	67
Family		5	2	7	84
Empty nester/no family		5	4	6	85
Post-family/retired		2	–	3	94

* less than 1%

Table 4.2 Consumer interest in skiing, 1993. *Source*: Mintel (1994).

Base: 25,832 adults	Watch on TV	Read reports
	%	
All	16.6	1.9
Men	17.2	2.5
Women	16.1	1.4
15–24	19.4	2.5
25–34	19.1	2.6
35–44	17.1	2.2
45–54	17.6	1.8
55-64	14.7	1.4
65+	11.8	1.1
AB	23.2	4.1
C1	20.0	2.2
C2	14.2	1.3
D	12.4	1.2
E	11.4	0.7
£35,000 or more	28.1	5.5
£20,000–34,999	23.0	3.1
£15,000–19,999	20.9	2.8
£11,000–14,999	17.7	2.4
£8,000–10,999	16.3	1.4
£5,000–7,999	14.0	1.0
£4,999 or less	11.8	1.2
Not stated	11.6	0.9

Table 4.3 Frequency of ski holidays by skill level. *Source*: Richards (1995).

Frequency of ski holiday	Level of skier		
	Advanced	Intermediate	Beginner
More than one a year	68	40	10
One a year	30	55	71
Less often	2	5	13
Total	100	100	100

4.2 MOTIVATIONS OF THE SKIER

One of the most interesting studies of skiing behaviour has been conducted by Mills (1985), who tried to determine whether or not the empirical structure of motivation for participating in downhill skiing corresponded to Maslow's theory of motivation. The author's justification for choosing downhill skiing to test Maslow's theory was based on the fact that many skiers report experiencing something similar to Maslow's description of self-actualization. A random sample of 708 visitors was interviewed at Tahoe, and respondents rated the importance of each of 23 items for having a successful skiing day. The upper four need levels in the Maslow model were operationalized for use with the Tahoe skiers. Mills hypothesized that an empirical structure existed that could be described by a mapping sentence stating that the population of downhill skiers evaluated the importance of a self-centred as opposed to non-self-centred personal orientation for the satisfaction of four needs for having a successful skiing experience (see Figure 4.1).

This existence of a two-dimensional partitioning of the basic needs is seldom cited in recreation literature, yet Mills concluded that the self-centred/non-self-centred dimension of Maslow theory is more important to consider than the needs hierarchy when attempting to differentiate downhill skiers on the basis of motives. Mill's study contributes to a better understanding of how the Maslow needs operate as motivational 'pull' factors within the context of downhill skiing.

Figure 4.1 Mapping sentence indicating hypothesized theoretical structure. *Source*: Mills (1985).

'The extent to which skier (x) evaluates the importance of:

FACET A: Personal orientation   FACET B: Psychological need

                                                 b1 safety

a1   self-centred   for the satisfaction of   b2 affiliation

a2   non-self-centred   b3 esteem

                                               b4 self-actualization

    HIGH

                   for having a successful skiing experience.'

    LOW

However, various 'push' factors through which many participants may be motivated to go skiing should also be included in motivational studies of skiing. Boon (1984) found that 'getting away from the usual demands of life' figured highly among benefits sought by skiers at Ski Beech in North Carolina (see Table 4.4). Boon found significant differences in benefits sought between various segments of the skiing population. He discovered differences between weekday and weekend skiers – the latter placed greater importance on such benefits as testing abilities, getting to know the lay of the slopes, and keeping physically fit – and between skiers of differing abilities. For example, he found that beginners placed a significantly higher amount of importance upon 'being near others who could help' than intermediates or advanced skiers. Benefits such as 'experiencing excitement' and 'leading other people' were more important to advanced skiers than they were to the other groups, whereas intermediate skiers placed greater importance on benefits such as 'being with other people who enjoy the same things you do'. Boon's study, by combining socio-demographic variables with benefits sought from the downhill ski experience, provided useful information for the ski market concerned, and highlighted the importance of market research. In an article for *Ski Area Management*, Fernald (1986) stated that 'while the ski industry on the whole is extremely sensitive to marketing, the segmentation of the market by ability level is, perhaps, under emphasised'. Similar studies of which benefits are sought could be conducted in Europe to provide managers of resorts with detailed customer information.

Table 4.4 Rank order of mean scores of benefits sought by skiers visiting Beech Mountain ski resort during winter 1983. *Source*: Boon (1994).

Benefit Factors	Mean Scores (n = 734)
1. Being with friends	1.498
2. Being with others who enjoy similar things	1.504
3. Getting away from the usual demands of life	1.539
4./5. Having a change from your daily routine	1.542
6. Keeping physically fit	1.583
7. Developing skills and abilities	1.586
8. Giving your mind a rest	1.688
9. Testing abilities	1.732
10. Experiencing new and different things	1.736

In a more limited segmentation study of skiers, which did not include benefits sought, Mills, Couturier and Snepenger (1986) segmented the Texan skier market into two groups, heavy and light spenders (determined by total ski-trip expenditure). These segments were differentiated from one another and from other Texans in terms of socio-demographic characteristics. Skiers were grouped according to their total expenditure for each ski trip and bisected at the middle point of the cumulative frequency distribution. Cross-tabulations were done between socio-demographic variables and three data groupings: heavy-half skiers (heavy spenders), light-half skiers (light spenders), and non-skiers. Statistically significant differences were found for several of the descriptor variables which made it possible to differentiate light- and heavy-half Texan snow skier segments from one another and from other Texan households. The results indicated that future studies should incorporate benefits sought and other relevant variables to provide a more meaningful segmentation of the skier market.

In a similar study, Goeldner (1978) segmented the Colorado skier market in terms of in-state as opposed to out-of-state skiers. He concluded that different marketing methods must be utilized to reach each segment since each differs in behaviour. He also acknowledged that a further breaking down and in-depth analysis of each these segments would result in better identification of important segments and better knowledge of how to communicate with them.

In 1989, the Ski Industry Association commissioned McKinsey & Company to review and analyse existing data on skiing and skiers ('McKinsey & Company' 1989). McKinsey divided the market into seven customer segments based on skiing frequency and inclination to ski. These were:

1. *Potential* never skied but have similar demographics to skiers;
2. *New* skied for the first time this year;
3. *Intermittent* consider themselves a skier, but do not ski every year;
4. *Light* skied 1–5 times last year;
5. *Moderate* skied 6–15 times, typically including a vacation;
6. *Heavy* skied 16+ times last year;
7. *Drop-out* consider themselves a former skier.

McKinsey concluded that heavy skiers held little additional potential and that the greatest future potential lay with the light skiers. McKinsey reasoned that light skiers had already made a commitment to the sport and that their frequency could be enhanced if certain improvements were made. These included: minimizing the hassle of getting to and from the slopes; improving the on-slope experience (especially by policing out-of-control and fast skiing in beginner areas); making skiing 'beginner friendly'; and investing in employee training.

Tikalsky and Lahren (1988), in reviewing motivational research for risk-taking sports, suggested a few hypotheses that could help explain skier behaviour. First, recreational activities often function as a form of social release, in which participants can temporarily behave in a way not constrained by usual customs and protocol. Second, many people (the majority of skiers, in their opinion) are involved in skiing for non-athletic reasons since the social benefits may be more powerful primary motivators. Third, for many non-athletic people skiing often functions metaphorically in that one can pretend to be a vigorous mountain person coming to grips with risk and danger. Finally, a high percentage of the skiing public is more concerned with safety and ambience than athletic challenge or risk. The authors concluded that the motivations for skiing are multiple, and that dangerous skiing is a complex social phenomenon.

Mintel (1996) compared the motivations for skiing with those for participating in other sports in (see Table 4.5). Skiing is distinct among other sports in terms of offering 'pleasant or attractive surroundings'. This benefit is the top motivation overall, although the social and family benefits feature highly too. Interestingly, very few (four and three per cent respectively) felt that one did not have to be fit for skiing and that it does not cost much, reinforcing previous research that indicated that skiing is perceived as costly and energetic.

Table 4.5 Reasons for going skiing and playing other selected sports, 1995. *Source*: Mintel (1996).

Base: 916 adults	Skiing	Swimming	Climbing	Golf
		%		
Pleasant attractive surroundings	68	5	62	46
Good social activity	61	26	41	70
Relaxing	35	48	48	55
For general fitness	20	58	45	22
Feeling of achievement	20	24	17	13
Competitive element	18	2	5	41
Do not have to be too fit for it	4	18	11	14
Does not cost much	3	28	28	4

In a recent article, Spring (1995b) analysed the 1995 National Skier/Boarder Opinion Survey and looked at how skiers in the United States are motivated to ski. He suggests that skier days could be 25–30 per cent higher if the industry were able

Figure 4.2 Relaxing in pleasant surroundings: key motivational factors for skiers.

to convince identified, on-the-slopes skiers, to ski every year. Table 4.6 shows the reasons provided for *not* skiing by those 24 per cent of skiers who were found skiing in 1994–5, but who did not ski in 1993–4.

Table 4.6 Reasons for not skiing. *Source*: Spring (1995b).

Reason	%
No time	22.5
Was not interested	21.4
Did not have the money	13.0
Did not get round to it	12.9
Different vacation	12.5
Health	4.9
Personal reasons	4.9
Had a baby	4.3
Safety concerns	3.8
Children too young	2.8
Environmental concerns	0.7
Other	15.4

Each of the barriers indicated by these reasons can be overcome, because somehow each skier was determined to get back on the slopes the next year. However, over 35 per cent of the identified, on-the-slopes skiers were staying at home or taking another vacation 1.7 out of every 5 years. Spring sees the base of hard-core skiers diminishing and being replaced by vacationers and families. He also points out the change in habits and attitudes of skiers as skiing becomes just another form of recreation, and believes that resorts need to broaden their winter offerings to communicate not only with a broader array of skiers, but with the winter vacationer, a much larger market than the skier market.

Williams and Dossa (1995) analysed survey results that were received from 12,862 skiers in 31 Canadian winter resort areas in 1994–5. They focused on the entry, drop-out and re-adoption patterns of skiers and snowboarders. The results are shown in Table 4.7. Their research indicated that the informal encouragement of friends as well as exposure to the sport as a child, were the most frequent ways in which today's skiers initially became involved with skiing. More formalized introductions through targeted programmes and local ski clubs acted less frequently as catalysts. The main reasons for dropping out were the combined effects of having children who were too young to ski, and financial barriers. Of those skiers returning to skiing after quitting, the largest proportion started again because they were able to get their children on skis. Many others returned to the slopes because of better financial circumstances and improved geographical circumstances. Younger skiers were significantly more influenced in their decision to return by the encouraging comments of friends. Williams and Dossa question whether or not the industry will ever really understand how to keep skiers interested and involved with the sport. Several basic motivations behind skiing have nonetheless been identified over the years, many of which were substantiated in this research. People ski for personal achievement, social reasons, enjoyment of nature, escape and thrill. In order to keep people from leaving the sport, there is a need to ensure the social benefits of skiing are not forgotten, as well as to address the financial constraints associated with skiing itself.

Lewis and Wild (1995) recently presented a model that provides a typology of UK skiers based upon level of skill and experience combined with behavioural and attitudinal aspects of skiing (Figure 4.3). In the model, the majority of UK skiers who call themselves intermediate are distinguished by their attitude and motivation to skiing. Both the recreational skier and the sports skier may be *capable* of skiing the most difficult runs, but the reason *why* they ski such runs will be totally different. A better understanding of motivational factors for different skier groups will help clarify the parameters of a typology of skiers suggested in this model. More importantly, it will provide a framework for the industry to identify more clearly targeted markets, and thereby providing much more efficient marketing information.

Table 4.7 Entry, drop-out and re-adoption patterns. *Source*: Williams and Dossa (1995).

	Male	Female
	%	
Form of introduction to skiing		
Started as a child	26.2	26.0
Live(d) near a ski area	7.0	7.1
High school or college club	10.4	9.6
Local ski/snowboard club	2.0	2.3
Friends encouraged me	31.0	30.7
My kids made me	3.5	4.1
Ever quit and started again	26.9	30.5
Reasons for quitting		
Children were too young	16.1	27.0
Financial reasons	19.5	16.4
Geographic reasons	15.9	10.7
Health reasons	5.7	8.8
Personal reasons	17.2	13.0
My spouse made me	8.4	7.9
Time considerations	2.7	1.6
Other reason	14.4	14.7
Reasons for returning		
Children now ski	24.2	33.1
Financial reasons	13.4	9.4
Geographic reasons	13.6	7.7
Health reasons	4.6	3.7
Time considerations	8.8	8.5
Influenced by friends	13.8	19.8
My kids made me	4.0	2.2
My spouse made me	2.7	5.0
Other reason	14.9	10.6

Figure 4.3: Typology of the UK Skier (Lewis & Wild, 1995)

Skier type	Frequency of skiing	Equipment-buying behaviour	Ski terrain
Expert	Every season; often a continual period of skiing for several months	Several pairs of skis/boots	All terrain, on- and off-piste, skilled in all snow conditions
Sports skier	Every year and often more than once a year	Skis: specialist forms, e.g. slalom or giant slalom. Boots: performance comes first, comfort second	All pistes but specializing in jumps, bumps, turns and moguls; challenge-seeking and technique-perfecting; still not confident in all snow conditions
Recreational skier	Generally one week per year but may not go every year	Skis: all purpose, easy turn. Boots: comfort first, some performance	Any pisted area: cruising pistes (includes 'bombing'); leisure-seeking
Novice	One week	Hires equipment	Nursery slopes

4.3 THE NON-SKIER AND CONSTRAINTS TO SKIING

Past market research in the skiing field has, as already mentioned, focused on existing skiers; parallel research concerning skiing's latent demand markets has been less evident. However, as concerns for a falling ski market have surfaced, so has interest in identifying potential markets that may be persuaded to ski (Williams and Hayden 1986). Such studies, although based largely on household telephone methodologies, have provided valuable insights into the constraints facing the non-skier. However, as Williams and Basford recognized (1992), these studies have failed to address the constraints associated with distinct sub-groups of the non-skier population, and the relative significance of the impediments to these segments. Kay and Jackson (1991) pointed out that it is often the relative strength of these constraints that will trigger decisions to participate.

The non-skiing population in the UK is quite substantial. According to Mintel

(1996), 83 per cent of UK residents (80 per cent of men and 87 per cent of women) have never skied (see Table 4.1, p. 69). Further analysis of this sub-group shows that the likelihood of skiing decreases with both age and social status. If, according to Mintel, the average British skier is in the ABC1, 15–34 category, then the 61 per cent of this group that have never skied, represent a high potential market. Williams and Basford (1992) segmented the non-skier population and found that the two major deterrents preventing respondents from participating in skiing were perceptions of the activity's dangers and costs (see Table 4.8). However, Mintel (1996), in its effort to discover reasons for not taking a skiing holiday from the UK, did not even mention dangers in its first two consumer questionnaires. To be fair, Mintel has drawn upon data from a survey designed to examine who buys ski clothing and who is interested in media coverage of the sport, and these data do not allow a serious examination of the constraints facing the non-skier. It is probable that, unlike Williams and Basford, Mintel did not support the questionnaire design with any qualitative research. Qualitative insights can help clarify constraint issues that would merit particular attention in a survey. Also, Mintel made no distinction between those who have never skied and those who have ceased participation. Rather, consumers were asked: 'Which of these statements best describe why you have not been skiing or not been skiing in the last five years?' The results, comparing the 1989 and 1993 survey with the latest 1995 survey, are shown in Table 4.9.

It is clear from these results that the most popular reasons for not choosing to ski were the lack of appeal and the expense factor. However, progress is being made to make skiing more attractive, even if the vast majority never go. Every year fewer people are giving negative responses towards the subject of skiing, and the proportion of adults expressing the negative view – 'skiing has never appealed to me' – has dropped from 49 per cent to 39 per cent. Even so, this is still the main barrier; these percentages include many people who can go abroad only once a year and who prefer a summer holiday (15 per cent) and, in more direct competition to skiing, those who prefer a winter sun holiday (11 per cent).

Mintel expands the report by examining, in each demographic sub-group, the top five reasons for not skiing. This provides interesting results *if* the constraints are genuine. The striking element in attitudes comes out of a comparison with the actual skiing population. Although the young and affluent (ABC1, 15–34) were shown to account for much of the core market, a high proportion of these, 35 per cent, say that skiing has never appealed to them, thereby taking themselves out of the market. As in other leisure constraints studies, no effort is made by Mintel to understand *why* skiing does not appeal to a group that probably has a high potential for conversion from non-skier to skier. From this data it appears that skiing is not

Table 4.8 Skiing constraints, ski image clusters average score overall and for social adventurer and young family separately. *Source*: Williams and Basford (1992).

	Overall Average Score*	Social Adventurer Average Score	Young Family Average Score
Danger/fear			
Skiing seems like a very fast sport	4.5	5.0	4.3
For someone who knows how, skiing is not dangerous	4.1	4.0	4.7
Afraid of being out of control	3.6	4.8	2.3
Ski hills are very steep	3.5	4.2	3.0
Skiers take more risks than non-skiers	3.3	4.3	2.9
Chances of serious injury are much less than 5 years ago	3.4	3.7	3.6
Ski-lifts are scary	3.1	3.7	2.3
Cost constraints			
Cost of equipment	4.7	5.1	4.8
Important to have easy, inexpensive transport to ski area	4.6	5.0	4.8
Skiing would take up too much time	3.2	3.4	2.6
Low-cost, all inclusive beginner's package would entice me to ski	3.0	5.0	5.2
Many take up skiing because it is glamorous/trendy	2.9	3.6	2.5
Difficulty			
Skiing is physically demanding	4.7	5.0	4.5
Skiing is harder to learn than other sports	3.3	4.3	2.5
Skiing is for younger people	2.8	3.0	2.0
Not sure how to learn to ski	2.7	4.1	2.0
Not enough information how to ski	2.6	3.9	2.4
Beginners look silly, I would feel embarrassed in front of friends	2.2	3.4	1.5

* 1.0 = strongly disagree, 6.0 strongly agree.

Table 4.9 Reasons for not taking a skiing holiday, 1989, 1993 and 1995. *Source*: Mintel, (1996).

Base: all adults who have never skied or have not done so during the last five years	1989 Base: 1311	1993 1728 %	1995 1860
Cannot afford/too expensive	34	34	31
Only one holiday a year and prefer to take it in the summer	15	18	15
There are too many other places to visit/ other holidays to go on	–	18	*
Too old to learn	15	15	10
Not fit/sporty enough	15	15	11
No one interested in going with me	10	10	8
Prefer a winter sun holiday	–	10	11
Too energetic/not relaxing enough	13	8	5
The family is too young to go skiing	7	7	*
Too much organization and additional expense	–	6	*
People who go skiing are not my type	7	4	4
Risk of no snow puts me off	–	2	*
Skiing has never appealed	49	44	39
Skiing is too dangerous	*	*	7
Too costly for the whole family	*	*	11
Other	6	10	8

* not asked

only concentrated among those who are young and affluent, but among a sub-group that is enthusiastic about the sport for more specific reasons. This reinforces earlier suggestions that skiing appeals to a certain type of personality as well as certain socio-economic groupings. However, these results should be received with caution. It is this author's belief that such a study should first divide the latent ski demand market into those who have never skied and those who have. The study should then be based on a more thorough research methodology before the implications are acted upon by the ski industry.

The Mountain International Opinion Survey (MINOS), referred to earlier, attempted to understand the reasons skiing numbers were shrinking in Europe (Spring 1996b).

A total of 24,003 surveys were completed in five languages and in 32 mountain resorts in France, Italy, Switzerland and Austria. According to Spring, the reasons cited for skiing less often sound like an echo of United States skiers who ski less often: number one reason is cost; number two is time and logistics; and number three is competitive activities in other parts of the world. Snow is extremely important to the European ski vacationer, but this has not been dependable over the last decade: without early evidence of snow, skiers are making other holiday plans. Spring continues to speculate about the cost and value of going skiing; he suggests that Europeans are thinking about alternative package deals that provide better accommodation, have more choice of activities, and feed an apparent hunger to experience adventure and exploration in other parts of the world.

Williams and Lattey (1994), following on from the previous study of non-skiers by Williams and Basford (1992), specifically analysed women and the constraints they face by using the original data from a large survey of non-skiers in western Canada. The study's findings describe some of the underlying conditions that keep women from skiing more often. In particular, the role of social setting, activity characteristics, and location features associated with the skiing experience are described from a constraint perspective. The authors suggest that the reasons why women are not more involved with skiing arise from their interpretation of what constitutes satisfying leisure and the types of constraints they associate with the skiing experience. Many women perceive skiing to be a physically challenging sport beyond their athletic capabilities, and they place greater emphasis on enhancing the emotional and social dimensions of skiing, as opposed to valuing the physical benefits. What makes skiing appealing to some women is the opportunity it offers for enjoyment of the outdoors, for the company of friends and family, for the chance to use one's time efficiently, and, to some extent, for skiing downhill under control.

Hudson (1998a) operationalized a contemporary model of leisure constraints in order to examine the constraints on skiing for both participants and non-participants. A qualitative approach was used to develop a questionnaire that could measure perceptions of intra-personal, inter-personal and structural constraints. A list of 30 constraints was developed directly from the results of in-depth interviews and focus groups, and this has been abbreviated for the constraints model in Figure 4.4. Analysis of the qualitative research revealed that non-skiers faced a number of intra-personal constraints. They perceived skiing to be harder to learn than other sports, and suggested that they would feel self-conscious or embarrassed learning to ski. They also thought the activity would make them cold and wet, and that it would be dangerous, expensive, and too stressful. There was a feeling that skiing is an élitist sport, and that they were not 'chic and glamorous enough' to go. Skiers, on the other hand, were constrained by time, family or economic factors. The author sought to build an instrument that would measure perceptions of intra-personal, inter-personal and structural constraints on skiing participation. The measure followed a format common in previous constraints research in which subjects were asked to indicate their strength of agreement with, or the importance of specific constraints on, a Likert-type scale (Henderson, Stalnaker and Taylor 1988; Jackson 1993; Raymore, Godbey, Crawford and von Eye 1993).

Since the focus of the study was on high-potential non-skiers as well as existing skiers, the sample was taken from a membership listing of a health club chain called Dragons in the south of England. This chain attracts mainly young, affluent, health-conscious men and women. ACORN profiles for each of the clubs were obtained by the author, along with demographic details for the clubs. (ACORN is one of the longer established geo-demographic household classifications.) These were compared to the demographics provided by Mintel (1996) for regular skiers and non-skiers, and also compared to the profile of a skier as suggested in 'Portrait of a skiing enthusiast' (1993) and by Greer (1990). A close correlation was found. The author chose the quota sampling technique, where sample members are chosen on the basis of satisfying a pre-specified criterion thought to apply to the population. The sample selection was linked to the overall objectives, and therefore had to be representative of both the UK skiing population, and of those considered to be high-potential non-skiers. Two and a half thousand questionnaires were given to the members of Dragons, based on the quota selection criterion set out above, and 412 (16.5 per cent) usable responses were returned and consequently analysed.

Table 4.10 Perceived constraints on skiing for all respondents.

Rank	Constraint	Mean	In Agreement (%) n=412
1.	Clothing and equipment are too expensive	3.754	296
2.	Anticipation of expense	3.551	267
3.	Lack of low-cost, all-inclusive holidays	3.488	222
4.	Prefer to take a holiday elsewhere	3.169	183
5.	Do not have enough money	3.148	202
6.	Others do not have the money to go with me	2.890	152
7.	The slopes are too crowded	2.795	99
8.	Concern about the lack of snow	2.767	115
9.	Too much hassle buying or renting equipment	2.633	116
10.	Too much planning involved	2.572	84
11.	Afraid of injury	2.534	113

Figure 4.4 Constraints to skiing participation. *Source*: Hudson (1998a).

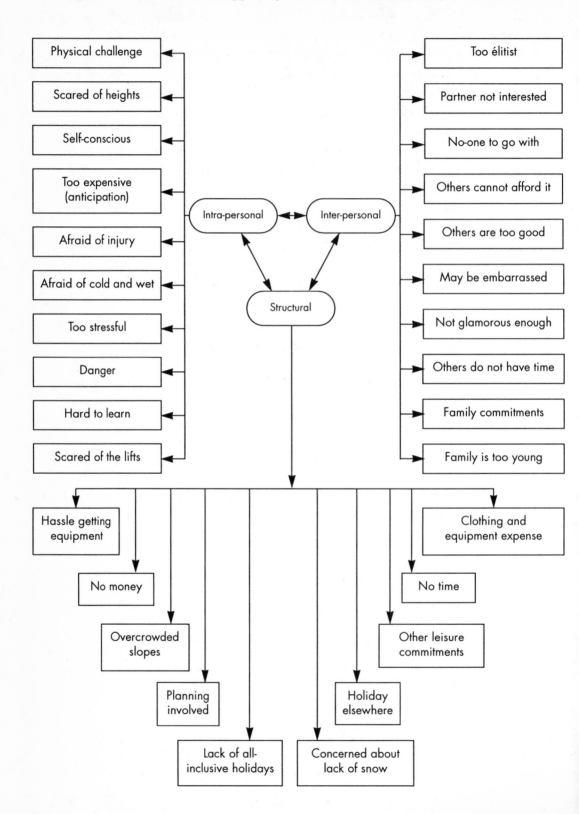

Analysis of the questionnaires indicated that economic factors were the major constraints for both groups. The ten highest scoring constraints are listed in Table 4.10. The fact that skiing clothing and equipment are too expensive is the number one deterrent, with 64 per cent of respondents agreeing with this statement. Hudson also compared skiers to non-skiers and found that 24 out of 30 constraints were rated significantly higher (p<.05) by non-skiers than skiers. The only constraint that concerned skiers more than non-skiers was the worry about lack of snow. This confirms the findings of previous researchers (Carmichael 1992; Richards 1995) who found snow conditions to be the key variable for existing skiers when making destination choices.

The means, standard deviations and differences in means for intra-personal, inter-personal and structural constraints are shown in Table 4.11. Using Levene's test for equality of variance, the intra-personal mean score for non-skiers (M = 2.46, SD = .69) was significantly higher (t = 6.70, df = 410, two-tailed p<0.01) than that of skiers (M = 2.05, SD = .69). For structural constraints the mean score for non-skiers (M = 3.16, SD = .50) was significantly higher (t = 8.03, df = 410, two-tailed p<0.01) than that of skiers (M = 2.72, SD = .58). Although the difference in means was the smallest for inter-personal constraints (.2620), the score for non-skiers (M = 2.36, SD = .64) was still significantly higher (t = 4.49, df = 410, two-tailed p<.01) than the score for skiers (M = 2.09, SD = .56). These results would tend to support the findings from the qualitative research, where non-skiers expressed a relatively large amount of intra-personal constraints in comparison to skiers.

Constraints for both groups were analysed individually. Skiers perceive just eight constraints, the major ones being economic. This suggests that skiers do not suffer from intra-personal and inter-personal constraints, or, if they do, that they have successfully negotiated them and do not perceive them as constraints. The fact that constraints *do* exist for this group supports the recent propositions that participants are also constrained (Kay and Jackson 1991; Shaw, Bonen and McCabe 1991; Wright and Goodale 1991). For non-skiers, skiing was perceived as expensive, and as not worth the effort involved in planning and organizing. Also, one of the top constraints for non-skiers was the fear of injury; this was also seen by Williams and Basford (1992) as a major constraint (although it was not enumerated by Mintel). Other perceptions by non-skiers are that the slopes are too crowded, that skiing is harder to learn than other sports, and that they will get cold and wet skiing. Non-skiers also see skiing as an élitist pastime. For some, or all of these reasons, many non-skiers prefer to take a holiday elsewhere, a constraint that featured highly in the Mintel survey.

Table 4.11 Differences in means for skiers and non-skiers.

Constraint typology		Mean	SD	Mean Difference
Intra-personal				
	Skiers	2.0501	.5687	
	Non-skiers	2.4680	.6970	.4179
Inter-personal				
	Skiers	2.0908	.5692	
	Non-skiers	2.3600	.6449	.2620
Structural				
	Skiers	2.7258	.5829	
	Non-skiers	3.1648	.5099	.4390

CONCLUSION

From this literature review, it is apparent that past research supporting marketing and product development programmes for skiing has focused primarily on gaining a better understanding of the socio-economic, attitudinal and behavioural characteristics of existing skiers. It is questionable whether or not the industry will ever really understand how to keep skiers interested and involved with the sport. However, several basic motivations behind skiing have been identified over the years. People ski for personal achievement, social reasons, enjoyment of nature, escape and thrill. In order to keep people from leaving the sport, there is a need to ensure the social benefits of skiing are not forgotten, and a need to address the financial constraints associated with skiing itself.

As concerns for a falling ski market have surfaced, so has interest in identifying potential markets that may be persuaded to ski. The non-skiing population in the UK is quite substantial, and current research suggests that the major constraints to skiing participation for these people are both intra-personal and structural.

CASE STUDY: MERISKI

An example of a company that has been successful in targeting and satisfying one segment of the skiing market is Meriski, a small tour operator based in Great

Barrington, Oxfordshire. The company was founded by Colin Mathews in June 1984, and initially developed as a lifestyle support system before becoming more of a business in the early 1990s. In November 1994 the company was bought by Brown Rock, who, apart from owning another chalet company – the Ski Company – owns and operates a group of bars, restaurants and nightclubs in the Alps. Brown Rock acquired the business from Colin Mathews and his partner Daniel Holmes for approximately £285,000, paid by way of new shares in Brown Rock. The position of Meriski in the group structure can be seen in Appendix 4.1 on page 90.

Meriski operates fourteen luxury chalet holidays exclusively in Meribel, France, and over the years has grown from 70 beds to 145 beds. Meriski is one of the largest chalet operators in Meribel, offering some of the best chalets for rent in the Alps. Meriski has consistently achieved occupancy levels of over 90 per cent, and for the year ending 30 April 1998 achieved 92.4 per cent on sales of £1.9 m. Projected profit and loss for 1998–9 is shown in Appendix 4.2 on page 90. The company also offers an Alpine hotel programme featuring top hotels in Meribel, Courchevel and Val d'Isere. It also runs a summer Alpine pursuits programme based in Meribel, which offers golf, rafting, mountain biking and canyoning.

Meribel has always attracted a particular type of British client. In fact it probably hosts the largest number and greatest proportion of British visitors of any European ski resort. There is a traditional reason for this in that had it not been for a handful of British pre-war skiers, Meribel would not have existed. In 1937 the impact of the war in Austria persuaded Major Peter Lindsay and a group of former Indian army skiing friends to look towards France, and Meribel in particular, to continue their favourite pastime. In 1938, after purchasing a few acres of land, Lindsay named the area Meribel after a nearby local hamlet, because of its better 'ring' in English than Les Allues, the French name for the valley. The first ski-lift soon followed, named the Red Dragon. It was a bus chassis with a winch in its engine hood and it carried nineteen skiers over about 300 yards. After the Second World War Lindsay developed the resort with the help of two main architects, Paul Grillo and Christian Durupt. The desire for traditional stone and wood buildings adhering to strict rules and regulations was paramount in the founding vision and is just as solid today. However, since 1936 the resort has grown from a mere 517 inhabitants to a massive 33,000 beds of all types. The total ski area, known as *Les Trois Vallées* is one of the largest ski regions in the world, interlinked by a highly sophisticated lift system. Some key dates in Meribel's history include the founding of the satellite ski village of Mottaret in 1972, just a year after Lindsay himself past away, and the creation of a major sports complex at the *patinoire* (skating rink) as part of the sixteenth Winter Olympic Games in 1992 when Meribel hosted the ice hockey tournament and the ladies' skiing events.

Meriski has capitalized on Meribel's popularity with the British. Since the inception of the company fifteen years ago, it has focused on providing the highest levels of customer service, and its team of 45 staff has to be prepared to embrace Meriski's philosophies towards the service culture. Each winter a team of managers is employed for five separate departments – crèche, driving, office, operations and guest services. A 1998–9 job description for services manager is provided in Appendix 4.3 on page 91.

Meriski considers itself to be a leader in the luxury holiday market, and it places an emphasis on targeting families in the ABC1 social classification groups (professional, senior and junior management). As a one-resort specialist, Meriski holds a unique position in the market. However, it has several strong competitors who offer a similar or slightly enhanced service in other top French resorts. Prices range from £399 to £1155 for a week's chalet holiday, but the average price is about £800, which includes return flights and transfers. Guests are flown to France via a charter airline, British Midland; in 1997–8 Meriski was guaranteed 132 seats each week on this flight.

For the 1998–9 season Meriski produced a 36-page glossy brochure. About 15,000 were printed for circulation, the majority going directly to existing and potential customers, who typically account for 80 per cent of sales. However, the company does sell 15 per cent of its holidays through agents who receive 10 per cent commission on sales. A sales presentation is usually made to these agents each season to ensure that they have the maximum amount of information about the product. The total communications budget for 1998–9 was approximately £50,000; its allocation can be seen in Appendix 4.4 on page 93. The £11,829 spent on advertising was divided between the *Sunday Times*, the Saturday *Telegraph*, the *Financial Times*, the *Daily Mail* ski magazine, the Marks & Spencer Magazine, and *Good Housekeeping*. A group press trip was scheduled for January to Meribel, with invitations sent to national newspapers, freelance ski writers and glossy magazines.

Future plans

A key marketing objective for Meriski is to ensure that Meriski is the best known name in the Meribel luxury chalet market. The marketing emphasis is on existing guests and agents, but it would like to attract new guests – particularly couples and groups, and preferably those who currently travel with competitors such as Mark Warner and Simply Ski. The corporate market has also been identified as a potential segment for growth, as it currently accounts for just 5 per cent of sales. Meriski has also recognized the potential of the Internet for marketing its products. Its current site has four pages – home page, chalet page, hotels page, special offers page and a brochure request form. There are plans to increase the size of the site to provide more chalet information with more pictures and floor plans. The special offers page is updated on a weekly basis throughout the season in order to attract as many callers as possible.

In a report compiled by the Constantinou Consultancy for Brown Rock, a SWOT (Strengths–Weaknesses–Opportunities–Threats) analysis (see Appendix 4.4 on page 94) was used to make suggestions for the future of Meriski. It was suggested that the Meriski chalet brand remain exclusively in Meribel as the brand is both established and strong. Despite the solid brand awareness and healthy client loyalty, it was recommended that both these strengths be improved upon by product and service alterations and a greater marketing focus. The exact number of properties under the brand remains flexible, but the consultancy believes that there is a need to operate a policy of 'top-end in, bottom-end out' in terms of chalet quality, in order to retain market niche and customer loyalty, and to keep ahead of the competition.

Appendices

4.1 Brown Rock Limited – group structure.

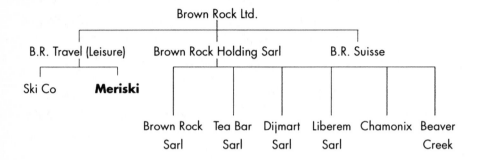

4.2 Meriski profit and loss for year ending 30 April 1999.

Expenditure/Income Types	£
Sales	1,363,900
Cost of sales	(441,649)
GROSS PROFIT	922,251
COS of sales (%)	(32.40)
Overheads	
Personnel costs	(155,574)
Motor and travel	(15,148)
Property rent	(7,862)
Utilities	(784)
Advertising and promotion	(49,661)
Stationery and printing	(9,348)
Housekeeping and general	(10,374)
Maintenance and repairs	
Insurance and bonding	(2,758)
Telephone	(6,068)
Professional fees	(15,028)
Book charges	(666)
Depreciation	(11,349)
Total Overheads	(284,619)
Overhead as percentage of sales	(20.90)
EBIT	637,632
EBIT as percentage of Sales	46.80
Profit before tax	637,632

[Bracketed figures indicate negatives.]

4.3 Job description for services manager 1998–9.

SERVICES MANAGER

Would suit: Customer services oriented person, with good organizational skills. Administration skills essential and experience with client liaison a huge advantage. Should be interested in problem-solving and staff motivation.

Regarding customer services:

- Organization of transfers to and from resort – holding weekly transfer meetings, in liaison with transport manager
- Maintaining customer service levels to the standard required – including operation of chalet visits
- Overall responsibility for customer complaints, problems and accidents – and the subsequent paperwork
- Reaction to questionnaire results, check-lists and subsequent weekly reports (and any other reports) to ensure the best and most satisfactory solution for our clients
- Liaison with the heads of all other departments and, via them, all staff, to ensure the best holiday for all of our clients
- Job description of GC (guest co-ordinator) when dealing with clients

Regarding administration:

- Communication HQ for resort – control of message books, working with office manager
- Control of manifests: translation, distribution, updating and filing
- Processing and actioning of client questionnaire
- Accounting for all monies collected from clients, e.g. lift-passes, ski schools, ski hire
- Responsibility for and accurate recording of all credit card payments made in resort
- Recording and chasing of all luggage left in resort
- General customer services administration and rotas for customer services personnel as required
- Preparation and completion of weekly reports, with accurate filing for future use

---

Regarding staff services:

- Maintenance of all staff records
- Preparation of monthly staff wages information for UK accounts department
- Preparation of all staff packs for new staff members and gathering of their information
- Liaison with insurance company for staff details and claims
- Processing of necessary staff paperwork e.g. E101s, etc.
- Organization and recording of uniform distribution
- GC staff direct management – motivation, support, redirection and discipline

Regarding office duties:

- Operating rotational cover of office with office manager

Regarding communications:

- Liaison with managers to maintain staff motivation and morale
- Ensure communication between Ops. team and chalet staff is at an optimum

All managers will be involved in staff training and will attend a weekly managers' meeting. All managers should be prepared to cover the office in an emergency.

4.4 Meriski communications budget 1998–9.

How budget was spent	£
Brochure	
Production costs	22 250
Mail house costs	4 614
General mailing costs	4 000
Direct mailings	
General costs	600
Agents	
Agents' entertaining	350
Christmas wine	400
Advertising	
Total schedule	11 829
Internet	(included in advertising budget above)
Corporate markets	
Literature production	1 250
General mailing costs	250
Presentation costs	200
PR	
Brochure launch	300
Association Press lunches	472
One-to-one lunches	180
Press trips	1 340
Individual press trips	250
Total	50 085

4.5 SWOT analysis of Meriski.

Strengths	**Opportunities**
Single resort strength	Increase product quality
Top brand	Product innovation
High customer loyalty	Market penetration
Good marketing	
Good sales staff	
Upper middle range	
Growing market	
High selling price	

Weaknesses	**Threats**
Single resort dependence	Many competitors
Increasing competition	Exchange rate
Decreasing differentiation	Price saturation
Quantity of seasonal staff	Economic climate
Quality of seasonal staff	
Climatic conditions	

CHAPTER 5

Destination Planning and Operations

INTRODUCTION

This chapter focuses on both the location and development of ski resorts, and the management and marketing of these resorts on both sides of the Atlantic. The physical conditions necessary for a successful ski destination are examined, and two scenarios for the development of tourism in Alpine areas are discussed. The professionalism of resort owners in North America is compared to the more unpredictable and fragmented efforts of European resorts; this is highlighted by the case study on the marketing of Whistler in Canada.

5.1 SKI-FIELD LOCATION

Ski-field location, perhaps more so than in any other type of tourism, is heavily dependent on appropriate physical conditions, namely a good snow cover and suitable slopes. Research has shown that concerns about the lack of snow are a major concern for skiers and non-skiers alike (Carmichael 1992; Hudson 1988a). According to Pearce (1995), two main factors are important with regard to snow cover – the length of the season and the reliability of the snowfall. Longer seasons (from four to six months) and more reliable snowfalls will yield a more satisfactory and reliable return on investment in plant and infrastructure, and this is closely tied to altitude. At higher altitudes (2000 m or more) the snowfall is generally greater, and the snow will remain longer owing to the low temperatures. Exposure to winds will also determine the amount of snow retention and the need for snow-packing equipment. Duration of the snow cover is also a function of latitude; similar altitudes in the French Pyrenees and the French Alps will experience different conditions. Martinelli (1976) stresses the need for early season snow cover, as this is when demand is often the greatest (over the New Year period in particular) and when the financial success or failure of many areas is decided. If the temperature is low enough, many resorts now have the snow-making capability to put down a base at the start of the season if the snow has not arrived.

The quality of the snow cover is also important, with skiing performance and enjoyment being related to the following parameters: density, temperature, liquid water, hardness and texture (Perla and Glenne 1981). Temperature variations will affect not only the quality of the snow, but also the comfort of skiers and the design of buildings. Sunshine is important for the siting of resort accommodation and is a significant factor in skiing enjoyment.

Resort ski-fields must offer a range of slopes to attract a variety of skiers. Sibley (1982) reports that novice slopes should be under 20 degrees, intermediate slopes 20–45 degrees, and advanced slopes 45 degrees or steeper. Experienced skiers will also look at the variety of runs available, and at the total vertical drop. A certain amount of flat, stable land must be available close by to provide adequate building sites. Considerable care must be taken in locating both the base and uphill facilities in order to avoid avalanche paths (see Figure 5.1). Many of the more modern resort developments (in France, for example) offer a variety of pistes, in terms of aspect

Figure 5.1 A cornice in Sauze d'Oulx, Italy – care must be taken in locating both the base and uphill facilities to avoid avalanche paths.

and difficulty. These pistes converge on a single reception area where the accommodation and other facilities are built. Such a design gives skiers immediate access to all parts of the ski-field.

A ski-field will be at an advantage if it links with other ski-fields. For example, Aime 2000 forms part of La Grande Plagne area, which in turn is favourably situated in the Tarentaise ski region of France. Proximity to summer resorts or attractions is another advantage, as the summer season becomes ever more important to ski resorts. Proximity to the market is also a key factor in influencing visitor numbers. Access and proximity to urban areas is especially important for resorts catering for day and weekend skiers, and this is the case for many North American resorts.

5.2 SKI-FIELD DEVELOPMENT

Ski-field development depends on the exploitation of natural resources, and a significant investment is required to provide the necessary uphill facilities. This, coupled with difficulties of access and sparse populations in many Alpine areas, has led to much outside participation in the development process (Pearce 1995). The literature on ski-field development is heavily oriented to studies from the European Alps; in an early classification of ski-field development in the French Alps, Preau (1968) concluded that in any situation three sets of factors intervene:

1. The state of the local community when development begins – its size, its dynamism, its facilities.
2. The rhythm of development – whether this coincides or not with the growth possibilities of the local community.
3. The characteristics of the site and the technical and financial possibilities for developing it.

In a follow-up article, Preau (1970) proposed two different scenarios for the development of tourism in Alpine areas. The first scenario refers to summer tourism in Chamonix in the nineteenth century (Figure 5.2). The diagram, reading from top to bottom, emphasizes local conditions and factors that have been modified by tourists discovering the attractions of the Alpine environment. The local society adapts to a diffuse and easily accommodated tourist demand. Urban developers from outside the area play only a gradual and complementary role, providing, for example, large hotels or capital for a mountain railway.

Figure 5.3 shows a completely different situation in Les Belleville in 1970, and the diagram reads from bottom to top. Development begins with the image of a functional resort conceived by urban promoters. It is no longer the mountains that are presented to tourists, but the developed facilities such as apartments and ski-lifts. The mountain is reduced to a technical analysis of its characteristics – capacity of the ski-field, construction possibilities, ease of access, etc. The only demands made on the local community are for its land and labour.

Pearce (1978) has proposed a more general two-fold classification based on the division of responsibility in the development process:

1. 'Integrated' development implies development by a single promoter or developer to the exclusion of all other participation. The concept of the integrated ski resort is now generally accepted in France.
2. 'Catalytic' development, on the contrary, occurs when the initial activities of a major developer generate complementary developments by other companies or individuals.

This difference in the division of responsibility influences not only the nature of the development process, but also the resort's location, form, and, to a certain extent, clientele. Pearce gives La Plagne in France as a typical example of an integrated ski resort. In 1960 the huge snow bowl above the town of Aime in the Tarentaise valley was a natural mountain wilderness. Today, it is in the heart of the ten-village complex that makes up the resort of La Plagne. The destination was developed entirely by the SAP (*Société d'Aménagement de La Plagne*), a development company formed by a group of Parisian banks. Integration is most evident in the form of the resort. All the accommodation is located at 2000 metres, high above the traditional settlements situated in the valley below, and the amount of accommodation has been calculated as a function of the capacity of the ski-field in order to avoid overcrowding of the slopes. In one of the satellite resorts, Aime La Plagne – which is shaped like a giant toblerone – integration is carried to the extreme, as a single gigantic complex accommodates not only 2500 people, but also houses a cinema, discotheque, restaurant and a full range of shops.

The local population in La Plagne has been effectively excluded from this development. However, the creation of such a large ski-field has allowed the communities to undertake more traditional developments around existing settlements further down the mountain, such as Montchavin at 1300 metres. In this broader context the high-altitude integrated resorts may be thought of as having a catalytical effect on the area as a whole. The entire area now boasts 113 lifts catering for 114,000 skiers per hour, and these skiers have a choice of 45,000 beds.

Catalytic developments differ significantly from the integrated ones. First, catalytic developments are usually grafted on to existing settlements. Second, the presence of existing dwellings, together with the multiplicity of developers and the less intensive nature of their projects, gives rise to a much more diverse and less concentrated resort than that which results from integrated development. The range

Figure 5.2 Preau's scenarios of Alpine tourist development: Chamonix type. *Source*: Pearce (1995).

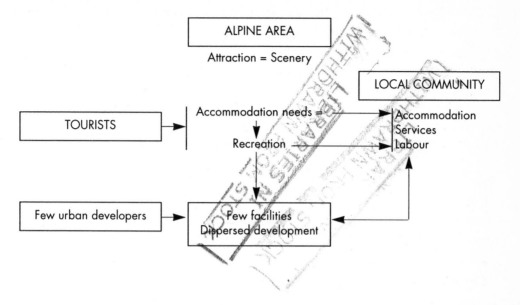

Figure 5.3 Preau's scenarios of Alpine tourist development: Les Belleville type. *Source*: Pearce (1995).

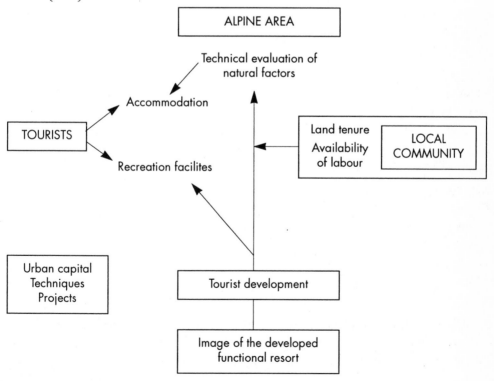

of accommodation types offered also broadens the base of the resort, and this may attract several different classes of visitor.

Barker (1982) identifies differences in scale, intensity and form of tourist development between the western Alps (France and western Switzerland) and the eastern Alps (eastern Switzerland, northern Italy, Austria and Bavaria). In the west, large integrated ski resorts were built in the sub-Alpine zone long after the local population had retreated to the main valley where agriculture, forestry and manufacturing provided employment. In these resorts, the main thrust for development came from distant urban capital. In contrast, tourism in the eastern Alps coexists with a strong pastoral economy. The impetus for development has come from within strong rural communities with a tradition of local autonomy in planning, and this has favoured community-based investment initiatives.

5.3 THE IMPACT OF SNOWBOARDING ON PLANNING

The invention of snowboarding has introduced an entirely new and conflicting recreation use to the slopes. In the process of expansion, snowboarding has created a growing number of perceived and reported conflicts for mountain managers. The urgency for management to understand and deal with this potential conflict has been exacerbated by the flattening in demand for skiing as a whole, and by the recognized need to restructure on-slope operations and products to ensure a continued flow of customers to the mountains. Williams, Dossa and Fulton (1994) have applied a multi-method approach to identify the susceptibility for conflict between snowboarders and skiers. Focus group information suggested that skiers perceived themselves to be more intimately involved with the resource base than were their snowboarding counterparts. Skiers characterized snowboarders as being primarily 'upstarts' who were intruding on skiing's pristine environment with little appreciation of its scenic attractiveness. They also suggested that the differences between themselves and snowboarders were most evident with respect to costume, language and on-slope behaviour. One focus group skier asked if the baggy clothes of snowboarders were used to conceal weapons!

Despite these differences, the authors concluded that the basis for potential conflict between snowboarders and skiers is actually quite limited. For the most part, specific on-site adjustments to the built dimensions of the mountainside product will help to reduce potential conflicts between these two groups. Indeed, traditional ski resorts have already begun to respond to the potential growth in conflict situations by creating snowboarder facilities and programmes. One example is the creation of on-slope snowboarding parks. These customized facilities are designed to create a more comfortable environment for snowboarders, and help segregate the two groups. However Williams *et al.* (1994) suggest that it is debatable whether, in the long run, segregation strategies will be the most effective way of dealing with potential conflict issues. Many skiers are adopting snow-boarding as a complement to their skiing activity, and it is unlikely that they would wish to be limited in their access to mountain areas they previously frequented as skiers. Similarly, most snowboarders particularly value the freedom to roam the mountain slopes at will. Attempting to enforce a segregation strategy that dilutes this feeling of freedom will only lead to *greater* potential for conflict.

Williams *et al.* believe that a more effective approach involves sensitizing resort staff and management to the requirements of the two groups. Through gaining a better understanding of the experience expectations of skiers and snowboarders, and having a clear mandate from management to respond to the needs of both groups, employees will be better prepared to offer visitors the kinds of experiences that each group expects to receive. Through such processes, skiers and snow-boarders, and those that manage their experiences, will create opportunities for mutual coexistence.

5.4 MANAGEMENT AND MARKETING OF DESTINATIONS

North America

North American ski resorts tend to be much more snow sure than their European counterparts, and the tree-line is often much higher (see Figure 5.4). Presently, there are about 800 ski areas in North America, down 22 per cent from 1025 in 1985. In total they generated 70 million skier days in the 1996–7 season. The 520 areas in the United States generated about 52 million skier days (Harbaugh 1997). Those numbers have been more or less constant for the last few years. The four largest resort groups in North America accounted for approximately 18 million of those visits (26 per cent). Harbaugh argues that this consolidation is motivated more by financial market conditions – low interest rates and high market valuations – than by industry changes. He suggests that the gradual decline in the number of ski areas is the result of increasing competitive pressures in a maturing market. The ongoing aggregation of resorts is the result of fear of competitive pressures in the merging market, offers of prices for ski areas that are hard to turn down, plus some retirement and estate planning concerns.

In the USA, snow sports participants generate more than $12 bn in the economy (Packer 1998). Taking into consideration the summer months, total economic contributions coupled with summer mountain-resort business jump to well over the $15 bn mark. The USA's biggest ski resort chains have been buying many smaller resorts, and investing in new hotels, ski-lifts and snow-making equipment. Three

Figure 5.4 Aspen, Colorado, where the tree-line is over 3000 m.

chains have even lifted themselves in stockmarkets in the past couple of years –
something previously unheard of ('Winter Wonderlands' 1998). A $315 m spending
spree has left Vail Resorts, one of the most ambitious companies, with 40 per cent
of the Colorado market, including the country's most popular resorts. Intrawest, a
Canadian company, owns resorts spanning the continent's mountain ranges, from
the Laurentians in Quebec to the Sierras in California. In November 1997, the
American Ski Company, which already owned six resorts in New England, spent
$288 m on a pair of resorts in Colorado and California. Even so, skiing remains
fragmented by the standards of the leisure industry – the largest company, Vail,
accounts for only 9 per cent of the market.

The big resorts have several advantages. They can afford to invest in all the latest
technology; their lifts are warm and capacious; and the guaranteed snow is neatly
groomed. Beginners can hop on moving walkways when they tire of taking tumbles.
The chains are also expanding the range of activities on offer, such as ice-skating,
sledging and dog-sledging, snowmobiling and tubing (the increasingly popular activity
of sliding down the slope on the inner-tube of a lorry tyre). The idea is to turn the
big resorts into full-fledged winter theme parks, and thereby to attract more
beginners and families to the slopes. *The Economist* ('Winter Wonderlands' 1998)
believes that this 'Disneyfication' of North America's winter sports looks unstoppable.

By broadening into accommodation, skiing lessons and other activities, the big chains also hope to capture more of the industry's profits. Historically, ski companies have been content to be little more than lift operators (as they still are in Europe), allowing local businesses to cream off most of the potential income. Even in the USA, the typical skier still hands less than 20 per cent of his holiday cash to the resort owners. Vail, by contrast, earns so much money from secondary activities that it can afford to stop charging for its lifts in the evening. It manages 6 hotels, 72 restaurants, 40 shops and over 13,000 condominia.

Money is also bringing marketing flair. The three publicly quoted chains have introduced loyalty programmes and flexible pricing. Vail, whose new boss, Adam Aron, was one of the pioneers of air miles, has a marketing budget of more than $20 m. The American Skiing Company has joint marketing agreements with Budweiser, Pepsi and Visa, and sends 300,000 copies of its 'snow' magazine to its regular customers. All these companies, with the help of the NSAA and the Ski Industry Association (SIA), are attempting to create a $57 million campaign to support learning to ski and snowboard programmes. The money would be raised directly from the industry, with larger companies paying more than mid-size and smaller companies, and would be used to select a top-flight advertising company to create and execute a media campaign that creates a heightened awareness of skiing and boarding.

Resort operators still earn a large chunk of their profits on the slopes, selling lift tickets, food and equipment. Intrawest has fourteen ski shops at Blackcomb, its flagship property at Whistler, British Columbia. However, property development and management have become an important part of the ski business. For the operators, the most desirable visitors are what the trade calls 'destination skiers' – travellers who spend a week or two at the resort, fill ski-lifts on otherwise quiet days in the middle of the week, and spend money on accommodation, meals, lessons and equipment. Resort operators are increasingly banking on these visitors to fill hotels, townhouses and condominia in the valleys below the slopes. Marriot, the US hotel chain, and Canada's C. P. Hotels will manage two new hotels at Intrawest's Mont Tremblant resort in Quebec (Simon 1996). Intrawest hopes the chains' resources and computerized global reservations systems will help keep the resort full throughout the week. The company are also looking to rapidly increase property sales, and Ralcorp and Intrawest expect to sell 200 units a year at Keystone Valley, a joint venture in Colorado. The operators benefit not only from selling townhouses and condos, but also by helping the new owners rent their properties to visitors. Typically, they charge a management fee equal to half the rent.

The biggest risk to such development remains the weather. In order to thrive without snow some operators have invested heavily in snow-making equipment.

They have also added non-ski activities, such as conference centres and golf courses for summer visitors. The aim is to complete a virtuous circle in which improved year-round facilities help attract property buyers, no matter what the weather.

An excellent example of a successful company that has benefited from the industry consolidation in North America is the American Skiing Co. Created in 1996, the American Skiing Co. has grown from being a strong regional ski company in the east to one that has a enormous presence in North America. With chairman Les Otten at the helm, the company now owns nine resorts: Attitash Bear Peak in New Hampshire; Killington/Pico, Sugarbush and Mount Snow/Haystack in Vermont; Sunday River and Sugarloaf USA in Maine; The Canyons in Utah; Steamboat in Colorado; and Heavenly in California. The company controls about five million skiers annually, or about nine per cent of the skier traffic nationally.

The story began with Otten's transformation of Sunday River from the backwoods of Maine skiing into an eastern powerhouse. He borrowed $840,000 to buy the financially strapped ski area from his employer, the Sherburne Corp., which also owned Killington and Mount Snow. Sunday River lost $235,000 on $541,000 of revenue in 1980, posting just 40,000 skiers. Otten made snow-making his top priority, and also built new lifts, trails, lodges, condominia and a quarter-share condominium hotel. Today, after investing more than $100 million in the resort, Sunday River has seen its annual skier visits increase to nearly 600,000, second in the east only to Killington.

As well as improving the quality and service in their resorts, the American Skiing Co. is actively expanding the base of skiers for the next century by recruiting teenagers as well as Europeans. In 1997 the company recorded 40,000 skier visits from the British market alone – a 50 per cent increase over the previous winter. Otten also hopes to diversify by attracting off-season recreation and hotel convention trade. The American Skiing Co. now operates the largest golf school in the east (The Original Golf School), boasts 18-hole championship golf courses at Sugarloaf, Sugarbush, Killington and Mount Snow, and offers a plethora of summer activities including lift-served mountain biking, guided hikes and scenic chair-lift rides.

Europe

The European winter sports market divides clearly into two (Spring 1996b). The southern countries of Austria, Switzerland, southern Germany and France and northern Italy represent about one-half of the skier population (fourteen million). Skiers from these countries have relatively easy access to the Alps, and buses from Vienna, Salzburg, Munich and Geneva haul ski clubs and students to the mountain resorts with regularity. The remaining half of the European market lives in the north. The bulk of this market is vacation market. Depending on the country, skiers from the north spend an average of six to fifteen days on a ski holiday. Most skiers from the north drive to the Alps, a trip that can take up to twelve hours for the British and seven hours for the Parisians.

Table 5.1 Resorts, beds and ski-lifts in France. *Source*: Barbier (1993).

Resorts	Beds	Ski-lifts
La Plagne (Savoie)	45 000	106
Chamonix (Haute-Savoie)	37 000	45
Serre-Chevalier (Hte-Alpes)	35 000	65
Courchevel (Savoie)	32 000	68
Les Arcs (Savoie)	28 500	71
Tignes (Savoie)	28 000	53
Meribel (Savoie)	28 000	47
Val d'Isere (Savoie)	25 000	49
Les Menuires (Savoie)	22 000	54

The French ski industry is characterized by very big ski resorts (see Table 5.1); for commercial reasons these resorts are grouped into two. Ski France, label of the Mayors' Association of French winter sports attracts 102 communities, and claims to have 90 per cent of the country's accommodation, 4000 ski-lifts and 30 per cent of the world's skiing area; France Ski International associates with the fifteen biggest French ski resorts – that is, one third of the accommodation. It is located in the northern Alps and its organization is supported by airline companies.

French resorts and tour operators in the UK have begun to adapt themselves, albeit a bit late, to progressive alterations in the market. The recent collapse of both the foreign and domestic markets of France have highlighted this necessity. For example, in 1996, to offset the effects of the strong franc, many operators increased their chalet stock in France; the logic behind this move was that if meals, afternoon tea and wine were included in the price, clients would not have to spend so much in the resort. Also, changing market demands have been recognised by the local ESF (ski schools) in resorts, which are looking to diversify into other skiing and related activities to broaden their portfolios (Lewis and Wild 1995). Improvements in transportation are likely to help the French business. In December 1997 a new Eurostar service started running from Waterloo International and Ashford International, taking over 700 skiers each week to Bourg St Maurice in the heart of the French Alps.

An interesting recent development in French skiing has come with the investment by Canada's Intrawest corporation into CAD, the world's largest ski resort operator, and owner of the French purpose-built resorts of Les Arcs, La Plagne, Les Menuires, Flaines and Tignes. Intrawest already owns both Blackcomb and Whistler mountains at Whistler Resort, rated seven times the number one destination in North America by North American skiers. As already mentioned, it is also developing integrated commercial/residential villages at North American resorts, and it may only be a matter of time before the same concept is applied to the French resorts.

The rise in popularity of Italy is linked to currency. The continuing strength of the pound against the lira is leading to forecasts of boom sales in sterling countries. Another area to gain from the pressure on the pound is Andorra. Tucked in the Pyrenees and straddling Spain and France, this tiny principality is traditionally seen as a budget, beginners' destination. But the ski appeal has been enhanced by bus links between the resorts to allow a much wider range of skiing. This has attracted the more advanced skiers.

Switzerland, Austria and France have struggled to keep market share, and hoteliers and tourist directors in these countries are at last recognizing the need to be competitive and to keep annual increases to a minimum, and are also dangling alluring incentives before tour operators. These range from cut-price accommodation to free lift passes and ski hire. For example, in 1995 Swiss tourism joined forces with seven UK tour operators to promote discount deals in the Jungfrau region.

Austria, which has held prices in recent seasons, is tipped to make a slight recovery. To win back market share, it has adopted aggressive marketing policies over the last few years. Leading the campaign is Top Ski Austria, a marketing alliance of the country's top eighteen ski resorts. The main aim of the group is to organize activities in selected markets that the individual resorts would not be able to achieve themselves. An 'Austrian Week' in 1995 in the UK attracted both trade and public, the objective being to reinforce the image of Austria by emphasizing atmosphere and après-ski. Austria, like Switzerland, is still perceived in the UK as more expensive than France, and positively prohibitive in comparison with Italy and North America.

Smaller ski destinations that may experience an upturn in British visitors are Norway, given a boost by the Lillehammer Olympic Games, and Sweden, which has just made a first-time appearance in a major brochure with Crystal Holidays featuring the resort of Are. Germany is likely to remain a minor ski destination for the British until it is able to cater for large-scale programmes; this may happen if it holds the Winter Olympics in the first few years of the twenty-first century. If resorts in Eastern Europe can overcome unreliable snow cover (by investing in snow machines), disorganized resorts, mediocre food and night life, and rising prices, then they, too, may attract an increasing number of British skiers.

Environmental awareness has had a big impact on skiing in Europe. In the Alps, the only new lifts for the foreseeable future will be replacements for existing installations. One future answer to ecological concern is to put ski-lifts underground. Saas Fee, Zermatt, Val d'Isere, Tignes and Les Deux Alpes already have underground funiculars. Other resorts are thinking of following the examples of Zermatt, Avoriaz and Wengen by forbidding cars in the resort. The Austrian village of Lech sets an example for the future with its policy of limiting the maximum number of skiers on any day to 14,000.

5.5 DESTINATION CHOICE

Product planning and positioning are important aspects of proactive marketing management for the tourism industry. Carmichael (1992) recognized that research focusing on the image evaluation of resorts by potential visitors will lead to greater marketing effectiveness. She studied the tourist image and destination choice conditions for a sample of downhill skiers who were residents of Victoria, British Columbia. Using conjoint analysis she provided information on the relative importance of attributes that skiers sought in ski destinations.

Using the aggregate and individual-part worth utilities computed from conjoint analysis, she measured and compared tourist images for the resorts that skiers were considering in their evoked sets. The overall importance of each attribute in its contribution to preference was presented diagrammatically, and it was interesting to see that snow condition was the key variable (way beyond any other variable) for skiers. Collection of image data for resorts in this way can form a preliminary step in model building and the prediction of tourist movements. In this study conjoint analysis was shown to offer a sound methodological tool for studying consumer perceptions and behaviour. The study could be further extended to an analysis of resort positioning through using variance and multi-dimensional scaling techniques.

In a more recent paper, Carmichael (1996) compared and examined different methods of market segmentation for their usefulness in targeting skier markets. Figure 5.5 outlines some of the variables that according to Carmichael, have potential as segmentation criteria. They include socio-demographics, behavioural factors and benefits sought either within the ski resort attributes or within the ski experience itself. In this study it was hypothesized that the importance that skiers place on ski resort attributes in the decision-making process of choosing between resorts was a sound basis for skier segmentation. Skiers were clustered on the importance they placed on ski resort attributes, as revealed by conjoint analysis.

Figure 5.5 Skier segmentation variables. *Source*: Carmichael (1996).

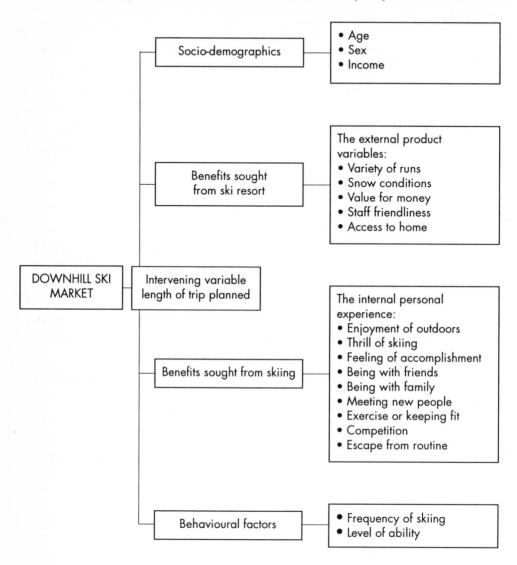

The segments were then compared on demographic, behavioural and motivation variables. A traditional, a priori approach to clustering found significant differences between segments for both short-trip and long-trip scenarios. For the short trip, four meaningful segments were identified:

1. *Variety lovers*: younger, higher skiing ability, strong need for accomplishment;
2. *Value lovers*: need to escape from routine;
3. *Snow lovers*: need to enjoy the thrill of skiing;
4. *Access lovers*: lower skiing ability.

For the longer trip, two segments were identified:

1. *Variety lovers*: advanced skiers, moderate need for competition, strong need to escape, little need to be with family;
2. *Snow lovers*: need to enjoy the thrill of skiing.

Dilley and Pozihun (1986) looked at the five ski resorts in Thunder Bay, Canada and tried to find out – through an attitudinal survey – what causes the Thunder Bay skier to prefer one hill over another. The study focused on the skiers' own perceptions of why they choose to ski where they do. The authors found that in most cases the pattern of responses showed no significant variation when considered in terms of age, sex, marital status and skiing experience. Overall, the Thunder Bay skier believes that he or she is most influenced by the quality of the actual ski experience, plenty of well-kept runs, and little waiting.

So what was uncovered by Dilley and Pozihun were those factors perceived as being important by the skiers themselves. In many cases actual skier behaviour accorded with those perceptions. In a more detailed study of this area, Ewing and Kulka (1979) compared a revealed and a stated preference approach for estimating the site attractiveness of Vermont ski resorts to weekend skiers. They found that the same site factors explain both attractiveness judgements of ski resorts and cognitive images of them. The two factor groups were perceived length and variety of ski slopes on the one hand, and perceived crowding and price on the other.

Keogh (1980) proposed that a skier's 'needs' (expressed in terms of what he or she hopes to find during the skiing experience) and ultimately his or her choice of resorts are related to the skier's motives for going skiing. Based on a study of the skiing population of Grenoble in the French Alps, he defined three major skier-types:

1. *The sporting skier*: attracted by the more physical aspects of the activity; tends to be younger and more concerned by the length of ski runs than the scenery in resorts;
2. *The 'contemplative' skier*: attracted by the aesthetic outdoor experience; tends to be older and accords more importance to the scenery of the resort;
3. *The 'social' skier*: enjoys skiing mainly for the opportunity to participate in an activity with friends or family.

The two major motivational groups of skiers, those seeking physical sporting (58 per cent) and aesthetic outdoor experiences (34 per cent), were found to differ significantly with respect to the type of resorts they frequented. The more sports-oriented skiers were found to ski generally in higher resorts, with a greater number of runs, greater height differences, a greater number of lifts and, correspondingly, higher priced lift tickets. Those seeking the aesthetic outdoor experience were more likely to visit the lower and more modestly equipped resorts with correspondingly lower prices. Only the distance of resorts from Grenoble was not shown to be significantly different for these two groups. Keogh's results do not mean that differently motivated skiers cannot satisfy their needs in the same recreation area. But the examination of the types of resorts frequented by different skiers did reveal motivations to have a spatial expression. Additional work of this kind should be carried out under different environmental conditions – for example, with skiing populations further removed from mountain areas – and more precise methods could be employed to measure skier motivations using absolute rather than relative scales.

Another interesting study focusing on active skiers was conducted by Klenosky, Gengler and Mulvey (1993). They examined a variety of factors in order to understand and explain behaviour concerning ski destination choice. These factors ranged from the relatively tangible attributes of products, to the intangible benefits, needs, and personal values people seek to satisfy through their choice behaviour. A logical framework and methodology for relating these tangible and intangible elements is provided by 'means-end theory'. The means-end approach focuses on why and how product attributes are important. The authors collected data during a ski show held at Ottawa, Canada in November 1991, and from the results they constructed a hierarchical value map (see Figure 5.6) that illustrated and summarized the links between attributes, consequences and values elicited during the interviews. Obviously there may be important differences in the means-end structures of skiers in different markets, and the analysis should also be applied to European skiers, but the methodology does have great potential for applied uses. Its application can help skiing providers to develop and evaluate advertising strategies, segment markets, and position products. For example, a strategy could be developed that emphasized the 'challenge and fun and excitement' associated with the runs at the resort or, alternatively, the unique 'social atmosphere and sense of belonging' associated with the friendly people who work and ski there. Klenosky and colleagues admit that an interesting future study would be to replicate the procedure with a sample of inactive skiers (i.e. those who have not been on a ski holiday in the last five years) or non-skiers: 'Such an analysis would be of considerable interest given the number of recent studies on leisure constraints behaviour' (1993, p. 377).

In a recent survey of 1400 UK skiers, Richards (1995) asked respondents to indicate the factors that influenced their choice of destination. Not surprisingly, skiers emphasized the quality of the snow. Over 60 per cent of all skiers ranked 'snow conditions' as the most important factor, although more experienced skiers were more discerning in their evaluation than intermediates or beginners. Skiers

Figure 5.6 Hierarchical value map for ski destination centre. *Source*: Klenosky *et al.* (1993).

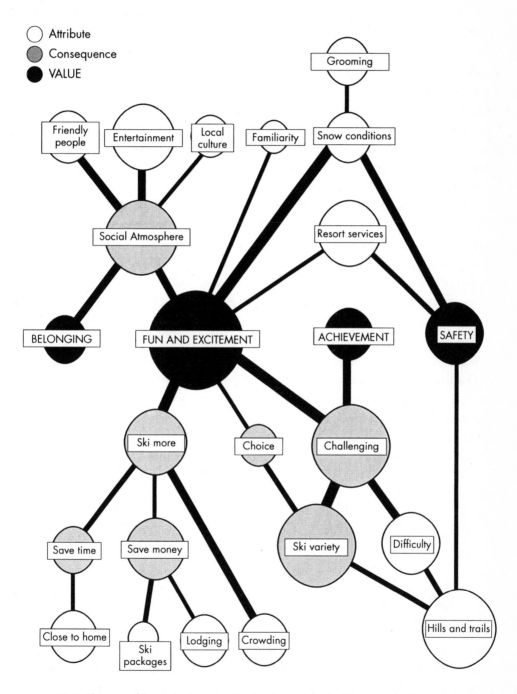

Note: The area of the circles is proportional to the number of subjects mentioning concepts.
The width of the lines is proportional to the number of subjects who associated the linked subjects.

were also asked to indicate whether they recognized certain countries and regions as ski destinations. Richards suggested that the areas that achieved the highest level of recognition were those that attract the largest number of UK skiers. However, looking at the table presented in his article (see Table 5.2), Austria and Switzerland, the second and fourth most popular destinations according to Mintel (1994), have been omitted.

Richards comments on the effect of marketing on destination awareness, seen from the high recognition of Colorado as a ski destination. Colorado has promoted itself relatively heavily in the UK market in the past five years, primarily through educating travel agents about the product and increasing coverage of Colorado in tour operators' brochures.

Customer destination choice will also be affected by the service quality provided by resorts. By identifying which attributes and services the ski market considers important, together with how well the ski resort provides these attributes and services, ski resort promoters can determine what the appropriate marketing message and strategy should be. This procedure, known as importance–performance analysis, was used by Uysal, Howard and Jamrozy (1991) and by Hudson and Shephard (1998) to identify and evaluate the attributes of ski resorts in North Carolina and Switzerland respectively. Basically, the procedure involves asking skiers to rate the importance and performance of identified ski resort attributes. Results are then graphically displayed on a two-dimensional 'action grid' that delineates weaknesses and strengths of the ski area in question (Figure 5.7).

Table 5.2 Recognition of selected ski destinations. *Source*: Richards (1995).

Country/region	Recognized by skiers as ski areas (%)
France	100
Italy	98
Bulgaria	84
Colorado	96
California	61
New York State	40
New Zealand	80

Importance–performance analysis is implemented in three distinct stages. Stage one involves developing a list of variables or attributes to be used in the study. Hudson and Shephard, rather than developing their own list from experience (as was done in the study by Uysal *et al.* 1991), conducted focus groups and in-depth

Figure 5.7 Importance–Performance grid with attribute ratings for ski destinations. *Source*: Hudson and Shephard (1998).

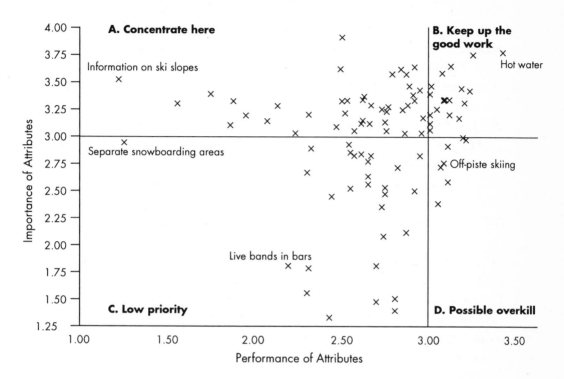

interviews in the resort, in order to produce a viable list of 97 attributes that served as the foundation for the survey instrument. Stage two involves conducting the survey to measure the product or service. Skiers were asked to rate the importance of an attribute in an ideal situation and then to rate the performance of the same attribute in relation to their experiences. In both studies, a Likert-type scale was used, with responses ranging from high to low levels for both importance and performance. The third stage is estimating the perceived importance and performance of each attribute through the calculation of the mean importance value and the mean performance value for each variable. The data is then presented on a grid where each variable can be plotted according to its perceived importance and performance. The graphical representation of the data necessitates that each of the attributes falls into one of four quadrants or cells: concentrate here, keep up the good work, low priority, and possible overkill. Figure 5.7 identifies where each of the 97 attributes in the Hudson and Shephard study fell in terms of the four quadrants, with an example pinpointed from each quadrant. Significantly, the largest number of attributes – 41, that equates to 42 per cent – was plotted in the 'concentrate here' (quadrant A) area of the action grid. Respondents rated these attributes high in importance but low in perform-ance in Verbier, Switzerland.

The findings of the study can be used by ski resort officials to develop potential management and marketing strategies. The procedure has great potential as a periodic monitoring device for detecting any shifts in skier satisfaction, and can be effectively used to point out a ski resort's strengths and weaknesses. The main limitations of the study lie in the survey instrument itself. The Likert scale does not have the ability to distinguish between subtle differences in levels of importance and performance. It also does not take into account any relationship that might exist between the *levels* of importance and performance and the *cost* of that service. In addition, inappropriate strategies may result from importance–performance analysis that excludes a dimension of competition.

However, the procedure is not intended to provide detailed and highly specific information. Should it reveal certain problem areas in terms of performance and expectation, more studies may be necessary to delineate exactly what the problems and concerns are and what the best possible solutions should be. Both studies reviewed did not attempt to consider possible intervening factors that may affect the composition of the action grid. Future studies could incorporate identifiable variables, such as the numbers of visits to the resort, skiing ability, and management styles in the resort. Further research could also differentiate between the responses of males and females, skiers and snowboarders, and independent skiers and those travelling with tour operators.

Both sets of authors found importance–performance analysis to be an effective tool in formulating and evaluating tourism policy in skiing destinations. The analysis of the data in the importance–performance grid was easily understood by the business community and helped facilitate the strategic planning process. As competition in the ski industry intensifies, and as more resorts around the world are able to meet customer expectations, excellent service quality will be determined by small details. Gaps in service quality will become smaller as the service provider becomes better at understanding the customer's perception of quality service.

CASE STUDY: THE MARKETING OF WHISTLER, CANADA

Tourism ranks fifth among Canada's export industries and contributed an estimated $27 billion to the economy in 1994 (Stokes 1996). In late 1994, Prime Minister Chrétien announced the creation of the Canadian Tourism Commission (CTC) which was given the task of marketing Canada. The grand plan was to involve all stakeholders – private industry and federal, provincial and municipal governments – in order to pool resources, talent and funds under one umbrella. Each stakeholder could then compete under that umbrella. Within a year of its conception, some $46 million in partnership funding was committed to the CTC. This boosted the marketing budget for the 1996–7 programme to more than $96 million.

One destination that has competed very successfully in this new marketing era is the mountain resort of Whistler. Canada has in abundance what tourists want, from raw wilderness for those demanding ecological and adventure travel, to polished cities for those in search of culture. And, of course, there are the mountains. Nestled in Canada's spectacular Coast Mountains, Whistler Resort is 120 kilometres north of Vancouver, British Columbia. From its early days as a little-known summer fishing retreat, Whistler Resort has become the country's most acclaimed recreational destination. Without the millions of dollars of marketing clout of certain big, US ski destinations, the resort is prospering through vision, tenacity and marketing savvy that is unequalled in the Canadian hospitality sector (Herzog 1996). Led by the Whistler Resort Association (WRA) – the worldwide destination marketing representative of the hotels, restaurants and shops at the foot of Whistler and Blackcomb mountains – the resort is positioning itself for continued success.

Over the past decade, Whistler has experienced unprecedented growth and rising stature as a world-class, year-round destination. Strong growth in visitor numbers has consistently been achieved in both summer and winter, year after year. In response to this success, the resort has undergone many changes. Huge increases in the number of accommodation properties (the resort has attracted investments totalling $550 million in construction over the past five years), retail shops and restaurants, along with extensive on-mountain improvements and expansions, have followed on the heels of the growth in overall visitor and skier numbers. These changes have improved the product offerings at Whistler, but they have also resulted in a temporary excess of supply over demand. Accelerated growth in visitor numbers is therefore vital, so that these new businesses will be viable in both the short and long term.

Whistler Village itself has a European influence, with gabled roofs and cobble-stone pathways. At the base of North America's largest ski area (7071 acres of skiable terrain), retail mingles with hotels, condominium developments and services. Since Whistler's establishment as a municipality in 1975, building investment has exceeded $2 billion. Now, with more than 20,000 pillows – 15,000 of those within 500 metres of the lifts – Whistler boasts the most ski-in/ski-out accommodation of any mountain recreation resort in North America. In the 1997–8 season, total skier visits reached 1.6 million, 7 per cent up from the previous year. The same winter, the number of room nights generated increased by 18 per cent to 448,467. The increase can be attributed to boosted visits from places such as Oregan (an 89 per cent rise), the US Midwest (65 per cent), the UK (54 per cent) and Germany (39 per cent). Origins of visitors can be seen in Appendix 5.1 on page 119.

For the first time, in the summer of 1996, the actual number of summer visitors exceeded that of winter visitors. This trend continued through the summers of 1997 and 1998. However, the value of the winter market continues to exceed that of the summer market. Winter visitors stay longer, spend more, and come from further abroad. When evaluating performance, based on the number of room nights generated, winter accounts for 57 per cent, and summer 43 per cent, of the total. This discrepancy is further amplified by an average winter rate that is approximately 60 per cent dearer than the average summer rate.

Over the years, Whistler and Blackcomb have each striven to match the other in size, service and facilities. This rivalry has resulted in an excellent lift system and visitor facilities. There is fast access from the slopes on high-speed lifts from five separate mountain bases. Indeed, out of a total of 32 lifts, there are 10 high-speed quad chairs and 3 gondolas. Both mountains are similar in size, offering a variety of terrain for skiing and snowboarding enthusiasts all covered by the price of one lift ticket. In 1997, when Whistler and Blackcomb merged under the ownership of industry giant Intrawest, the rivalry between the two resorts disappeared. The company invested more than $24 million on Capital Plan for the 1998–9 season, which included a new quad chair-lift for the Peak, the remodelling of the summit restaurants on Whistler, and a renaissance of the Creekside base area. Expansion is planned over the next five years at Creekside. A mountain neighbourhood will be planted at the base of the gondola, and plans have been drawn up for a carefully landscaped village. Buildings are to be in traditional architectural style, in order to preserve the spirit of the community and its history.

The non-profit Whistler Resort Association was formed in 1980 and is unique in that it is a legislated membership organization that is empowered to market Whistler. The WRA is responsible for developing co-ordinated strategies in the areas of sales, advertising, media relations and promotion of the entire resort. This responsibility includes the operation of a central reservations booking service as well as an activity and information centre. The association is also responsible for the operation of the Whistler Conference Centre and the Whistler Golf Club.

The association comprises three sector groups – accommodations, commercial business and ski operators on the two mountains – and representatives from each serve on the board of directors. An all-member meeting takes place annually to review both long-range and short-term visions. Involving Whistler's 9,000 full-time residents in the marketing process has been vital in achieving community cohesion and effective operations, and residents play significant roles – staging annual events as diverse as the Winter Start Festival, the World Ski and Snowboard Festival and the Whistler Summit Series.

WRA's vice-president of marketing and sales, Barrett Fisher brings extensive media experience to the organization, and with Fisher's explosive popularity, media enquiries have increased dramatically. In 1996, the media relations department handled more than 1500 enquiries and hosted more than 600 journalists. In the last decade, winter product marketing has expanded considerably. Whistler initially reached to the Pacific Northwest, eastern Canada and California through print advertising, but marketing activity has been extended to cover eastern USA and the midwest, New Zealand and Australia, Japan, Germany and the UK. The Canadian ski resorts have an impressive presence at the *Daily Mail* Ski Show in London.

The mission statement for the WRA marketing department (which appears on the first page of the WRA 1999 Marketing Summary) is 'to work closely with key strategic partners and take a leadership role in developing targeted and effective marketing programs that increase tourism to Whistler for the benefit of all WRA members'. Building partnerships has been essential to the WRA's marketing objectives, and, working with organizations such as the Canadian Tourism Commission and the Ottowa-based Tourism Industry Association of Canada (TIAC), the group has been able to maximize efficiencies. In some overseas markets, for example, Whistler is promoted as part of British Columbia's Golden Triangle, along with Vancouver and Victoria. A North-American free phone line and direct-dial service from Vancouver help position the destination as accessible and world class. The WRA also co-operates with Canadian Pacific Hotels and Delta Hotels to produce joint promotional material, especially for its growing conference business.

The importance of strategic partnerships is clearly demonstrated throughout the 1999 business plan. Each department has a number of partnership activities planned, which involve external, industry, and in-resort partners. For example, the research department works with the accommodation sector to produce monthly business performance reports. Key statistics generated by this project include year-on-year comparisons of room nights generated, average daily rates, revenue per available room, booking sources, travel type, area of origin of guest, and house and paid occupancy rates. Demographic profiles of Whistler's seasonal visitors can be seen in Appendix 5.2 on page 120. There are also some new and innovative partnership activities planned within the WRA that include integrated participation between departments.

However, the WRA's marketing team of 25 people does most advertising and promotional material in-house to give it greater control over its image and costs. The group also regularly conducts customer surveys to gauge satisfaction levels, identify areas that need improvement and formulate strategies. One area in which the group is attempting to improve is Whistler's appeal as a summer destination. Currently, average occupancy for this time of the year runs at about 43 per cent – relatively high for a predominantly ski destination. However, the WRA is keen to increase this figure, and many of its promotions (particularly directed at the USA and Germany) now focus on the destination's 'soft-adventure' appeal.

The WRA's strategies and tactics for 1999 and beyond are both to build upon successful campaigns and patterns from the past, and to incorporate new initiatives and directions. These strategies focus on building the year-round success of the resort by smoothing the peaks and valleys through targeted, timely programmes. The three main marketing objectives are: to achieve growth of 10 per cent in both winter and summer; to continue to diversify the market base by developing new market opportunities; and to attract high-yield customers with longer lengths of stay and high daily spending. However, the future presents challenges as well as opportunities for the marketing of Whistler Resort. Some of the challenges that will colour the first few years of the new millennium include: the economic situation in Asia (as well as the poor British Columbia economy); continued competition for a limited skier base; extremely competitive airfares into Colorado from key markets; and the need for growth rates to offset the increase in available accommodation.

Appendices

5.1 Whistler's hotel markets' area of origin.

| | Room nights (%) | |
	Summer 1998	Winter 1997–8
Canada		
British Columbia	44.1	25.3
Ontario	7.6	7.7
Alberta	2.1	3.1
Quebec	2.3	1.1
Other Canada	2.6	0.7
Total	58.7	37.9
United States		
Washington	12.1	10.5
California	6.8	6.6
Oregon	0.7	0.8
New England	1.4	1.7
Middle Atlantic	2.1	2.8
South Atlantic	2.9	2.6
Midwest	3.4	2.2
Mountain states	1.8	2.5
Southern states	2.4	3.2
Other USA	0.2	0.6
Total	33.9	33.5
Europe		
United Kingdom	2.6	12.2
Germany	1.4	1.8
Other Europe	1.0	0.5
Total	5.0	14.5
Other International		
Japan	0.9	10.3
Australia/New Zealand	0.4	2.3
Other countries	1.1	1.5
Total	2.4	14.1
TOTAL MARKET	100	100

5.2 Demographic profiles of Whistler's seasonal visitors.

Base	1130 Summer 1998	1569 Winter 1997–8
		%
Gender		
Male	53	66
Female	47	34
Age		
Under 25	8	14
25–34	22	30
35–44	27	29
45–54	24	20
55+	19	8
Household income		
<$50,000	17	24
$50,000–$74,999	19	18
$75,000–$99,999	28	17
$100,000–$149,999	22	20
$150,000+	14	22
Previous visitation		
First-time	47	45
Repeat	53	55
Household composition		
Married with no children	34	27
Married with children	39	26
Single, no children	25	42
Single, with children	3	4
Length of Stay		
Average number of nights	3.4	5.7

CHAPTER 6

Business and Environmental Conflicts

INTRODUCTION

For a growing number of skiers, the sport encompasses a great dilemma and conflict: between recreational enjoyment of the countryside and the conservation of the fragile Alpine and mountain areas where skiing inevitably takes place. The situation is particularly acute in the Alps where, in recent years, the issue has been given a high profile by many concerned environmentalists. This chapter looks at the impact of skiing on the environment and at the emerging concept of sustainability. The author then provides a model for the greening of ski resorts that shows the relationships between the key interest groups – tourists, operators, conservation groups, marketers, developers, management and legislators – and their varying influences on the resort's environmental policies. The model is operationalized using Verbier in Switzerland as a case study.

6.1 IMPACT OF SKIING ON THE ENVIRONMENT

As the tourist industry moves into the twenty-first century it will face the increasing problem of achieving not growth but rather a quality of tourist experience that is consistent with sustaining both physical and social environments (Ryan 1991). With an increasing number of conferences and publications dedicated to 'responsible' or 'alternative' tourism, it appears that academics at least are addressing the key environmental issues arising from the impacts of modern tourism. The mountains are among Europe's most threatened wildernesses (see Figure 6.1), and the rapid growth of skiing is central to this crisis. Skiing, in both practice and infrastructure, is causing numerous environmental problems that consequently give rise to serious challenges for the winter sports industry. In fact, a major deterrent to the further development of the ski market comes in the form of growing environmental concerns about human and traffic congestion in the mountains, and the intensive use of natural resources by skiers. Sager (1996) believes that environmental awareness, however perceived, will have the greatest impact on skiing in our lifetimes, especially in the Alps.

The Alps account for one quarter of the world's total tourism revenue. An estimated 100 million people visit the Alps each year and with them have come the problems of pollution and erosion. Despite its apparent strength, the Alpine environment supports a very fragile ecosystem. Any human impact is felt twice as strongly there as it is lower down in the valleys. Destruction has been caused by deforestation; by the alteration of use of traditional Alpine land for construction of dams, skiing facilities and hotels; and by the dumping of waste, which has polluted nearby lakes. Though tourism has saved whole facets of Alpine culture and economy since the last century, death by tourism and over-development is one of the major threats hanging over the Alps.

The continual use of the same location and of the same runs, together with the pressure to expand the skiing areas, has brought skiers and conservationists into conflict. Unfortunately, there is no way of compensating for the damage done on

Figure 6.1 The environmental impact of human traffic in the mountains is causing increasing concern.

the ski slopes and it is often permanent rather than temporary. In the long term, the face of the landscape changes and the whole ecosystem is altered. It is not just a matter of physical destruction in the forms of erosion, deforestation and the disappearance of rare habitats. There are also the problems created by car pollution and litter, and by the building of ski-lifts, cable-cars, new roads to allow coaches up the mountains, and avalanche fences. In March 1981, close to the purpose-built resort of Les Arcs, heavy rain and warm weather caused a small stream to turn into a torrent, destroying roads and bridges. Resulting landslides were responsible for many deaths, and repairs ran into several million pounds. The blame was put on tree-felling and the bulldozing of mountains to make pistes.

Also in France, there was much publicity about the heavy long-term ecological price paid for all the development undertaken for the 1992 Winter Olympics (Keating 1991). The natural environment may never recover from the frantic construction and massive injection of funds the games brought about. The men's downhill piste in Val d'Isere and the women's downhill in Meribel will leave scars on the landscape that will take hundreds of years to heal. The bobsleigh run at La Plagne was plagued by controversy, having been built on unstable, marshy land. To make it usable, it was frozen with 40 tonnes of ammonia, a substance normally banned by French law for use in public places. Local residents were issued with gas masks to protect themselves against poisonous fumes.

There are also environmental problems caused by artificial snow. The Alpine lakes source four major European rivers and their enormous hydroelectric potential is already widely exploited by ski resorts. Over 5000 snow cannons consume vast quantities of water, using 2.8 million litres of water for each kilometre of piste (Grabowski 1992). This artificial snow melts slowly and reduces the already short recuperation period of Alpine grasses and flowers during the summer months. Reduced river currents restrict upstream movements of trout, and there is a greater exposure of fish eggs to freezing.

There is a growing view that the landscapes of the western Alps in France, Switzerland and Austria are under serious threat from tourism, especially in the form of development of higher resorts. The growing tendency for the Alpine pastures, and the pistes with them, to deteriorate could be attributed to the loss of peasant farming that traditionally, maintained the ecological balance and conservation of the natural beauty of the Alps. The very important mutual links between land use, forestry, landscapes and tourism can only be maintained if the people who manage the landscape, the peasant farmers, are encouraged to remain in the mountains (May 1995).

Statistics documenting the tide of vacationers flooding into the Alps mask significant regional variations in the structure of the tourism industry and variations in economic importance. The statistics also obscure differences in cultural values and political organization that determine the actions of governments and host populations (Barker 1994). In the French Alps, the regional economic development policy of the central government over the last 30 years has resulted in the construction of urban-style ski stations with high bed capacities. The Tarentaise for example has a quarter of a million beds and the most dense concentration of ski-lifts in the world. Such stations are physically, economically and culturally divorced from the farming communities in the valleys. Inevitably there is a price to pay. The skiing facilities with hotels, lifts, car-parks and roads leave a network of impermeable water surfaces where water collects instead of gradually draining away.

In Switzerland and Austria, on the other hand, mountain agriculture and tourism have coexisted in a symbiotic relationship that has been strengthened by federal subsidies fostering local participation and control. But the issue of responsibility towards the environment is one that skiing authorities sometimes seem reluctant to accept. Some are even unwilling to admit the fact that skiing can damage the environment. Economic motives prevail, and the fear of losing business prevents them from making changes that could alter the whole nature of the sport. Unfortunately, bottom-line considerations have too often ruled over aesthetic ones.

Barker (1994) has highlighted some of the key issues in growth management in the Alps. She suggests that growth management and consolidation strategies tend to evolve through four phases along a learning curve:

1. An initial focus on quantitative growth witnessed in the 1960s and 1970s.
2. A shift in emphasis towards qualitative growth in response to market competition, sectoral problems, and emerging social and environmental impacts.
3. A recognition of the need for change once congestion becomes unacceptable to hosts and guests.
4. A fundamental reorientation in an effort to break out of the uncontrolled growth spiral. Integrated regional management strategies focusing on sustainable development concepts and the defining of limits aimed at ensuring socially and environmentally compatible tourism.

In her article, Barker gives three examples from the Austrian and German Alps to illustrate a range of strategies being used to contain tourism's growth. She believes that over the past two decades there has been a major shift from local, piecemeal solutions towards comprehensive regional management frameworks. However, mechanisms must still be developed to deal with trans-boundary problems, such as transit traffic and acid rain, that affect the existence and quality of Alpine tourism.

North America, too, has become more aware of the environmental impacts that skiing can impose. Environmental regulators often impose fines on resorts, and sometimes close them down for irresponsible practices. Even the father of theme parks proved no match for the earth's self-appointed guardians. In the early 1960s Walt Disney conceived a grand project for a giant ski resort between Los Angeles and San Francisco, complete with a fake Alpine village. Environmental lawsuits swiftly put a stop to the plans. For the ski industry, the environment and the industry's relationship with the Forest Service is going to be a more important issue over the next ten years than it has been for the last twenty (Leiweke 1996).

If the regulators do not impede development, then conservation groups certainly will. In October 1998 Vail in Colorado suffered $12 million worth of fire damage at the hands of an environmental group called the Earth Liberation Front. This occurred just two days after the first trees were cleared for a controversial expansion, which is intended to bring another 1000 acres of runs for skiers. Environmentalists have expressed concern about the threat to the habitat of the lynx. An extended public enquiry was held *vis-à-vis* the expansion, with Vail Resorts working closely with environmentalists before the project was given the go-ahead.

Another example of stringent planning permission comes from Vermont where Killington's plans to interconnect its ski area with neighbouring Pico Peak have been delayed pending an appeal by a local landowner over the water-withdrawal agreement. Also, Sugarbush had to link its two sections via a unique up-and-over chair-lift, the Slide Brook Express, to prevent skiers from disturbing the local bears.

An American ski magazine now presents the annual Golden Eagle Award to honour resorts that are environmentally friendly. The winner in 1998 was Aspen, Colorado, which has improved energy efficiency by heating some buildings with used motor oil, and which runs the new Cirque ski-lift with wind-generated electricity.

6.2 A MODEL FOR THE GREENING OF SKI RESORTS

A 1994 Roper survey on environmental attitudes in the United States found that public concern for the environment is very high (National Ski Areas Association 1994). Media attention given to the greenhouse effect, acid rain, oil spills, ocean pollution, tropical deforestation and other topics has raised public awareness about environmental issues. The survey discovered that skiers, especially, are worried about the environmental results of development and growth. Universal concerns regarding growth and development (such as traffic, adequacy of utility infrastructure, and effects on air and water quality) are now beginning to focus specifically on ski areas and their impact on surrounding communities. In the US

Figure 6.2 A model for the greening of ski resorts. *Source*: Hudson (1995).

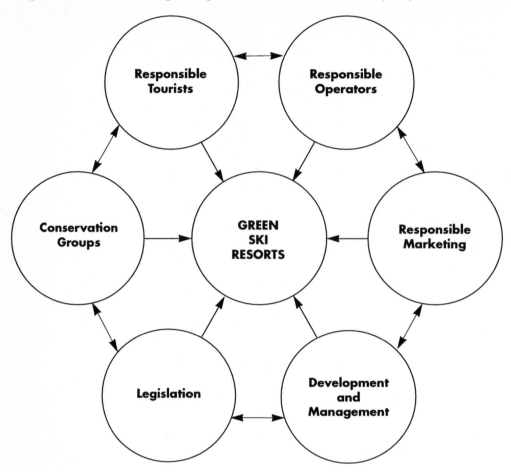

several dynamics have combined to create these environmental attitudes. Children are now educated on conservation and preservation subjects and are taught to respect the environment. Younger people are moving into positions of authority with agendas to protect resources and enforce environmental regulations. Also, corporate USA has jumped on the environmental sensitivity bandwagon, and companies have become 'green marketers' of their environmental commitment.

If skiers are genuinely worried about the environmental impacts of development in the Alps, and resorts accept that sustainability is the only way to survive into the twenty-first century, then the 'greening' of resorts must be the goal. There are several variables that contribute towards effective greening of a destination, and these can be represented in a model (see Figure 6.2) showing the relationships between these variables. The strength of these relationships will differ from resort to resort, and the power of each group of variables will vary depending upon the region and the country in which the resort resides. While each of the variables in the model will affect the greening of ski destinations in varying degrees (single-headed arrows), each will also influence one other (double-headed arrows). The relationships can be summarized as follows:

1. *Responsible tourists–responsible operators* The responsible tourist will demand a greener product and will look for the operator that can provide such a package. The responsible operator in turn can persuade skiers to travel with them for environmental reasons.
2. *Responsible operators–responsible marketing* The operator can use sustainability as a marketing tool and will seek to cooperate with resort marketers in order to communicate the right message to the consumer or media.
3. *Responsible marketing–responsible development and management* Marketers will be expected to keep management informed as regards to consumer tastes, attitudes, desires, etc. Management and developers will look to the marketers to inform the public of environmental efforts and use sustainability as a marketing tool.
4. *Responsible development–legislation* Management and developers must comply with any local, national or EC laws and, in turn, may lobby for rights to conduct their business in a responsible manner.
5. *Legislation–conservation groups* Conservation groups will use the existence of legislation as ammunition when exerting pressure on resorts. They will also lobby for new environmental legislation to curb irresponsible development.
6. *Conservation groups–responsible tourists* Conservation groups will influence tourists through the media and the tourists, in turn, may join, and even form, such pressure groups.

The influence of each variable is discussed below.

Legislation

Although the Alpine ski industry is generally acknowledged to be mature, there are increasing concerns about its sustainability. In 1991 the European Union established an Alpine Convention that aims to safeguard and protect the Alpine region and its ecological balance, threatened by growing human intervention. In the document, signed in Salzburg, the Alpine States and the EEC agreed on a framework convention for the protection of the Alps. By signing this document Austria, France, Germany, Italy, Liechtenstein and Switzerland committed themselves to cooperating on a strategy for development based on environmental goals. The Union now requires that before major developments take place, there should be an assessment of the potential impact upon the environment, and the Alpine Convention stresses the need for signatory nations to put measures in place that will protect the environmental resources of the Alps.

Legislation will also affect ski operators, and organizations may find in the future that greening is no longer an optional activity, chosen with a view to improving one's competitive position. If the industry as a whole does not act decisively soon, it may find that greening is imposed through government and supra-governmental regulation. The EC Package Travel Directive may well be an indication of legislation to come that will address green issues in tourism (Swarbrooke 1994).

Conservation groups

Membership of environmental organizations is growing. There are 2.2 million members in the National Trust and 250,000 in Friends of the Earth. Surveys show that 60 per cent of the public are sympathetic to environmental initiatives, while only 4 per cent actually oppose them (see Lane 1992). The media are largely pro-green, and tourism has been receiving increasingly critical coverage.

In North America a variety of interest groups – ecologists and conservationists, farmers and ranchers, small retailers and fishermen, senior citizens and historic preservationists – is finding common cause in fights to preserve communities' 'quality of life' (Beaudry 1991). More often than not, that common cause is opposing more resort development in communities' own backyards. From New Hampshire's Loon Mountain expansion to Colorado's proposed Mt Catamount, shocked developers everywhere are finding their way barred by newly discovered environmental red tape.

As ideas filter over from North America, similar concerns are also being voiced in Europe. Green Flag International, a Cambridge-based environmental group set up in 1990 with support from tour operators, is closely tracking the environmental impact of the tourism industry in the Alps. Haid (1989) talks of community 'Alpine emancipation groups' that use voting rights to oppose local political leaders still committed to tourism expansion. For example, Lausanne in 1988 was the first town to have a referendum on whether to make a bid for the Olympic Games. They rejected the event on environmental grounds. This was an acute embarrassment for the International Olympic Committee whose headquarters happen to be in the same town. More recently, both Davos and St Moritz voted overwhelmingly against submitting a bid for the 1996 Winter Olympics. At the moment, many groups in Switzerland are not happy with plans to bring the 2006 Olympics to the Sion Valley, despite the organizers' promises to have a 'balanced' games, reconciling the games and the environment.

Mountain Wilderness, an organization established in 1987 and known as the 'Greenpeace of the Alps', has dedicated itself to raising awareness of environmental problems and to the prevention of further damage. It has succeeded in stopping the building of constructions such as the ski circuit of Mount Pelmo, ski-lifts on the Chavière glacier in the Vanoise and a ski resort at Saleve.

Community action is not limited to defensive stands, especially when outside assistance is available. In the Bavarian Alps, for example, one commune of 5000 inhabitants has gone into partnership with Alp Action – a Geneva-based conservation charity chaired by Prince Sadruddin Aga Khan – to provide synergy between Alpine tourism and agriculture. The Prince writes of this and other initiatives in a recent book on ecotourism edited by Cater and Lowman (1994). In this particular area, the 'Hinderlang Nature and Culture Land', the entire community, along with Alp Action, has created a fund to help the farmers manage the environment. The farmers in return have signed an agreement whereby they will abide by a set of strict rules drawn up by environmental specialists and approved by the community. Elsewhere, Alp Action has planted hundreds of thousands of trees in six Alpine countries with the support of Jacobs Suchard International. This project is to encourage and perpetuate traditional mountain crafts by restoring some of the oldest Alpine chalets. And it has encouraged Clarins, a multinational cosmetics firm, to purchase land on behalf of the Swiss League for the Protection of Nature, in order to create Alpine butterfly sanctuaries. In fact, since its launch in 1990, Alp Action has contributed to the implementation of many environmental projects with the support of its 25 corporate partners in conservation.

Development and management

In addition to the higher incidence of citizen interest and participation in the planning process of ski resorts, more specialized jurisdictions and agencies are becoming involved in the approval of ski area development (Beeler and Wood 1990). Local sewer and water authorities; state agencies with responsibility for ecology, wildlife and cultural resources; and federal authorities governing wetlands and threatened and endangered plant and animal species – all may have a role in the approval of ski area development.

The Aga Khan has campaigned for closer consultation and co-operation between the mountain communities, state tourism, transport and industry authorities, and competent environmental experts. When planning ski resort development, destinations should work with all interested parties in a team effort in order to find mutually satisfying approaches to development. Much can be gained through open discussion with the interested parties, particularly those who are ski resort critics or development opponents. If issues of concern identified by local communities, environmental advocates or other recreationists are brought out into the open, this information can be used to develop a stronger and more unified plan, rather than

EMS Element	Component	Example action(s)	Example document
Policy	Purpose	Identify ski area's core values. Set broad goals for ski area sustainability.	Mission statement
	Commitment	Build senior management support and communicate it to staff. Identify environmental champions.	Statement from ski area president. Allocation of financial resources to EMS.
	Policy statement	Document ski area's commitment to environmental principles. State goals.	Copies of policy statement in employee newsletters, on trail maps, etc.
Planning	Analysis	Analyse ski area's environmental effects, its stakeholders, and regulatory requirements.	Formal scientific studies or informal inventories. Stakeholder correspondence. Regulations log.
	Objectives and targets	Set measurable targets that correspond to each policy objective.	Documented objectives and targets
	Implementation plan	Determine EMS scope. Develop a schedule. Assign responsibilities.	Plan document

Figure 6.3 Example of ski-area EMS implementation activities and products. *Source*: Todd and Williams (1996).

EMS Element	Component	Example action(s)	Example document
	Organization	Ensure that the organizational structure, including rewards and penalties, reflects accountability for environmental goals. Communicate expectations.	Revised organization chart. Revised job descriptions. Revised bonus scheme. Revised performance evaluation forms.
Procedures and controls	Performance measurement	Develop performance indicators and a monitoring schedule. Use laboratory tests and accounting information.	Records of test results. Analysis of cost savings.
	Information management	Document knowledge of key personnel. Write manuals. Incorporate results of performance measurement into a management information system.	Environmental and sustainability issues' library. Environmental operations manual. On-line access to environmental performance records.
	Incident response	Consider all risks. Develop a strategy and document it.	Emergency response manual
	Staff training	Identify gaps in knowledge and skills. Develop a training strategy using in-house and external resources.	Training courses and material. Seminars. Attendance at conferences.
Training and education	Research programme	Assess research needs and develop short- and long-term strategies.	Research reports. Improved training materials.
	Guest education	Educate guests about ski area environmental issues. Solicit their help.	Interpretive programmes. Guest feedback forms. Signage to reinforce environmental messages.

serve as a stumbling block during the approval process (Beeler and Wood 1990).

As already mentioned, more economic, social and environmental concerns should be addressed in the approval of ski-area development projects. But these issues are increasing in their complexity. Rather than planning on a piecemeal, project-by-project basis, ski areas need to consolidate their planning efforts in order to reduce the amount of negotiating required to gain approvals. Approval of a long-range master plan for development insures that step-by-step implementation of individual projects will go smoothly.

Todd and Williams (1996) have proposed an Environmental Management System (EMS) 'self-improvement' model for the North-American ski industry. They group the main elements of an EMS into six categories, and Figure 6.3 describes examples of actions and documents that might comprise an implementation plan for ski areas. The benefits include reducing the risk of penalties and financial liability for environmental damage; improving public and customer relations, reducing operating costs; and improving access to lenders, insurers and investors. Their analysis of North-American ski areas suggests that many resorts are currently involved in a wide variety of initiatives to protect and enhance their environmental resources, and that many of the proposed EMS elements are being used. Of these elements, communication programmes appear to be the most developed, while documentation has the most room for improvement. They suggest that employees, directors and stakeholders need to be educated about the potential for environmental degradation, especially in terms of cumulative effects. This will require the development of strong environmental education programmes targeted at all ski-area personnel; these are not currently in place in most ski areas.

Responsible operators

According to Wood (1992), a large responsibility lies with tour operators and the skiing industry itself: they should be seeking alternative places to send their clients, and also limiting the numbers present in any one season. She suggests that clients ask operators whether any type of monitoring is carried out; whether the company takes any active role in researching environmental damage caused by skiing; and, generally, what solution the company might offer by way of improving the situation.

Unfortunately, UK ski operators show little concern for the impacts of skiing on the environment. Very few have a financial investment in the host destination, and this means that their vested interest in the long-term sustainability of the destination product is low (Ryan 1991). Alp Action surveyed ski operators who were members of the Association of Independent Tour Operators (AITO), a group that has always stressed its green credentials. Out of 29 companies, only one had an environmental policy and none had heard of Alp Action and its conservation projects to improve the mountain environment. At a 'Tourism Society/Tourism Concern' conference in London in April 1995 on sustainable tourism, delegates agreed that the industry could not be trusted to regulate itself, and they called for government intervention to protect host destinations from operators tending to 'use up and move on'.

However, for many operators sustainability could be a useful marketing tool. It will cost a little more, but will help maintain, or even increase, market share in the long term. Ski companies could follow the example of the UK operator Eurocamp, a mass-market operator carrying over 40,000 families from the UK each year. Its main brochure carries a full page on environmental issues and describes the company's response to such issues. Before departure, clients receive detailed briefing packs outlining simple steps they can take to reduce their impact on the ecosystems of their destinations. On arrival, information is provided on locally made products, fauna and flora, environmental and community issues, and excursions on foot and by public transport.

Unfortunately, many companies in the skiing industry do not – and cannot afford to – think of the long term, and do not even consider environmental issues. However, there may come a time when they cannot afford to ignore them.

Responsible tourists

Can consumers be expected to put pressure on the operators to provide a greener product? A US Travel Data Centre survey has found that travellers, on average, would spend 8.5 per cent more for travel services and products provided by environmentally responsible suppliers (Travel Industry Association of America 1992). Kiernan (1992) reports that reliable statistics about the environmental consciousness of UK tourists are hard to come by. In Canada it is estimated that 40 per cent of consumers consider the environmental track record of both holiday company and destination when booking a holiday. Kiernan believes this figure to be about 10 per cent in the UK but growing rapidly. Other figures from the European Tourism Institute claim that more than half of all travellers are willing to pay up to 20 per cent more for a holiday in a natural preserved environment. The growth in special-interest, nature-orientated travel in the United States certainly reflects the increasing concern for the environment. Data on the US ecotourism market sub-stantiates this growth (Hawkins 1994). US tour operators report that between four and six million Americans travel overseas for nature-related travel each year. These operators say that 63 per cent of the travellers would pay $50, and 27 per cent $200, towards conservation of the area visited.

Wood (1992) suggests that skiers are starting to ask more questions about the environmental policies of companies they travel with, and that they believe that it would not take too many people refusing to book with irresponsible companies before changes would have to be implemented. However, Holden (1998) has discovered that in Scotland younger skiers – and they make up the majority of the market – are more emphatic in expressing their desire for fulfilling their needs through skiing even if they know skiing can damage the environment. These skiers are most likely to support the enlarging of a ski area, least likely to stop skiing even if they know skiing can damage the environment, and least likely to visit a resort if they cannot ski there.

6.3 RESPONSIBLE MARKETING OF SKI RESORTS

In the past ten years, just as manufacturers have labelled numerous products as 'green' or 'ecologically friendly', ecotourism and sustainability have become buzz words used to sell a variety of tourism products. The problem has been that the consumer has not known what he or she was getting, what the product's impact on the environment might be, and how the product differed from others.

Wight (1994) identifies the need for a balance between commitment to environmentally responsible action and commitment to environmental marketing. A destination can be sold as green, but false claims should not be made. The destination should be developed sensitively with regard to the long-term future, and consumers must be made aware of the genuine concern for the resources concerned. This position should involve more than the idea of balance, which implies compromise and trade-offs. It should involve the complementary integration of economic goals and environmentally responsible or conservation goals. Conservationists should consider the implications of *not* developing further: land already under pressure will suffer more severely as greater numbers of skiers compete for limited slopes, and habitats that have survived so far are likely to be irrevocably damaged.

Wight has provided a model to analyse the balance of commitment to both environmental improvement and environmental marketing in relation to tour operators. Hudson (1996) has adapted this model to position ski destinations based on their commitment to responsible marketing (see Figure 6.4). Four examples of destinations from different countries were put forward, and each takes up a different position on the model. The French purpose-built resorts have already been discussed (see Chapter 5), and a case study of Verbier follows at the end of this chapter (see pages 137–430).

At the Winter Olympics in 1994, set in Lillehammer, Norway, the organizers set out to market the first 'green' Games. Acknowledging the negative impacts major sporting events can have, the organizers used sport, culture and the environment as the three pillars that formed the foundation philosophy of the Lillehammer Winter Olympics. They appointed executives responsible for environmental issues and invested extra time and money in an attempt to make the Games the first in which the environmental challenge became an equal partner to the high profiles of sport and culture. As many people as possible were brought into the environmental programme, from schoolchildren to industrialists who could translate work done for the Games into marketable environmental products or services. The resort is now marketed as 'environmentally friendly', although not as aggressively as it should be, as resort officials are not totally convinced that consumers would rather visit, and perhaps pay more for, an environmentally friendly ski product.

A further example of the commitment towards the environment comes from Vail, where an innovative new programme, called Ske-Cology, allows young skiers the opportunity to learn about wildlife while skiing (Nelson 1995b). Skiing with instructors who have been trained to present the wildlife information, kids stop at

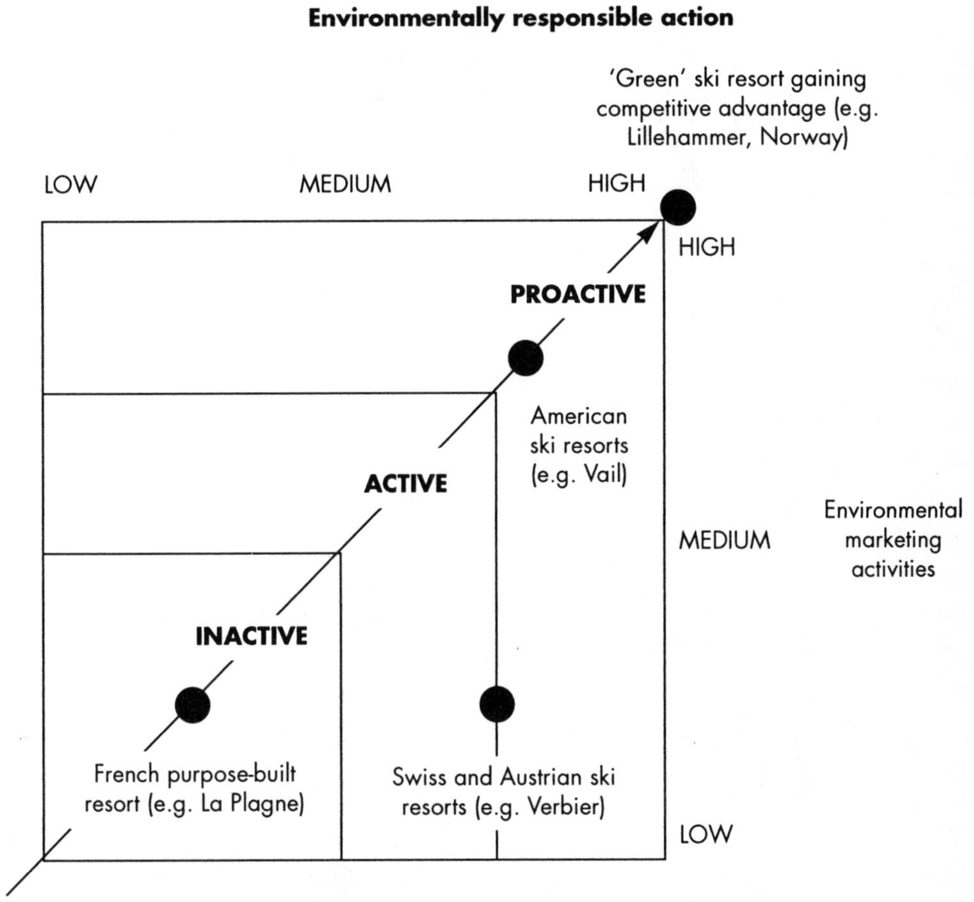

Environmentally responsible action

'Green' ski resort gaining competitive advantage (e.g. Lillehammer, Norway)

| LOW | MEDIUM | HIGH |

HIGH

PROACTIVE

American ski resorts (e.g. Vail)

ACTIVE

Environmental marketing activities

MEDIUM

INACTIVE

French purpose-built resort (e.g. La Plagne)

Swiss and Austrian ski resorts (e.g. Verbier)

LOW

Figure 6.4 Ski destination positioning for environmental activities and environmental marketing. *Source*: Hudson (1996).

signs along the trails to learn how animals and trees adapt, and how ski areas, in turn, adapt trail designs and tree-cutting to the forest ecosystem. There are now plans to extend the programme to include an adult version. This may not be such a bad idea, considering the results of a recent Snow Country survey. The investigation by Fry (1995) asked skiers, environmentalists and ski-area operators their opinions about specific issues affecting development in the mountains. Fry was not encouraged by the environmental knowledge on which these groups based their opinions, and concluded that inflammatory arguments over development in the mountains will not disappear unless ski-town residents, environmental protectionists, skiers and area operators better understand the environmental and economic facts and how and why groups think differently. The recent problems in Vail, referred to earlier in the chapter (see page 125), highlight these misunderstandings.

Figure 6.5 The continued constructions of pistes brings conservationists into conflict with resorts.

CONCLUSIONS

Despite growing environmental awareness, both ski resorts and the skiing public have a long way to go before they really understand the benefits and necessity of sustainable development. Until this education is complete it will be difficult for a destination to gain competitive advantage by marketing itself as 'green'. Researchers told environmentalists at the 1998 Climate Summit in Berlin that the majority of Europeans still cannot tell the difference between global warming and ozone depletion. Most believe that global warming is actually caused by holes in the ozone layer – presumably on the grounds that the holes let in more sunshine. (Global warming, a much contested phenomenon, is actually linked to the increasing levels of certain gases in the atmosphere that affect the absorption of outgoing terrestrial infra-red radiation.)

Such findings have implications for developers and resort marketers in the world's ski destinations. If they are to seize on the latest environmental buzz words (and 'sustainability', it could be argued, is one of them), then they must ensure that their employees and customers understand the meaning of the words. It makes sense to use the fact that 'green sells' for marketing purposes, but only when the product labelling conforms with both consumer expectations and industry standards. Lewis and Wild (1995) claim that some European resorts have already picked up on the potential advantages of using conservation (of environment or tradition) as a selling point that appeals to an ever-growing number of 'green' skiers. However, the author found little evidence of this, and even in North America, according to the NSAA, ski resorts that have laudable environmental programmes often fail to communicate their success to employees, skiers, the general public and especially the media (National Ski Areas Association 1994).

Holden (1998) believes that the ability to develop a skiing industry that is both market competitive and environmentally sustainable will be difficult, and that this is likely to place skiing in continued confrontation with conservationists and other mountain users (see Figure 6.5).

CASE STUDY: APPLICATION OF THE MODEL FOR THE GREENING OF SKI RESORTS IN VERBIER, SWITZERLAND

Two hours drive from Geneva, and close to the Italian border, lies the popular Swiss ski resort of Verbier. From a small farming community in the 1930s, Verbier has developed into a thriving tourist destination, with over a million overnight stays each year. The resort has 15,000 beds divided between hotels, chalets and apartments. A history of the resort can be found in Chapter 2.

From the first festival of Alpine herdsmen, organized in 1805 near Interlaken, tourism in the Swiss Alps has always been a part of an existing settlement scheme or land use system (Messerli 1987). However, during the 1960s and 1970s the exponential growth of tourism in the mountain regions resulted in a physical and economic predominance of tourism in many places, including Verbier. The important investments were mainly oriented to the winter season, in order to increase the rate of return. During this period tourism became the leading industry for mountain areas, and many now have a total economic dependence on tourism.

The Swiss Man and Biosphere programme (1978–85) made clear that this unbalanced growth has not only increased the risk of economic failure but also exacerbated the danger of disintegration of the local socio-economic–ecological system. Agriculture was identified as the most important linkage element in this system. As the basis for cultural identity, it also reproduces the traditional landscape, and this is found to be a formula for ecological stability, biotic diversity and recreational qualities. Messerli therefore believes that sustainable development of Swiss mountain tourism requires the integration of mountain agriculture with socio-economic development. He suggests that sustainable development in a changing socio-economic and natural environment should be based on three principles: prevention (environmental policy), flexibility (supply structure) and quality (personal services). Messerli highlights two significant events from the 1980s that affected Swiss mountain areas: first, the stagnation of tourist demand (indicating a saturation of the market in winter sports); second, some dramatic changes in the natural environment, such as floods, forests dying and a lack of snow. He believes that these two challenges call for an immediate transformation of the old, quantitative strategies toward a more qualitative and innovative orientation within further development. This not only implies structural adaptation in many resorts, but also a better regional co-ordination of further investments. Being an old and established resort, Verbier for one, is a ski resort that must face up to these challenges. Is 'greening' the answer? By applying the model for the greening of ski resorts referred to earlier in this chapter (see Figure 6.2), one may be able to draw some conclusions.

Legislation

The Swiss government was one of the first to adopt a policy of qualitative growth (the second of Barker's four growth phases, as discussed on pages 124–5). The Swiss Tourism Concept introduced in 1979 was aimed at restructuring and slowing down the rate of tourism growth and established an administratively binding framework for cantonal planning. But the policy and its implementation have been sharply criticized for the widening gap between stated objectives and reality. Jost

Krippendorf (1986; Krippendorf, Zommer and Glauber 1988), in particular, attacked the policies of many resorts, including Verbier. He suggested that the only solution is 'Alpine recycling', or the active reduction of over-capacity and assisted liquidation, rather than the continued subsidization of marginal operations. He believes that resorts sell their soil and their labour too easily – economic motives always being the strongest.

The Aga Khan (Sadruddin 1994) is in agreement with Krippendorf, and believes that competition must be frozen in the field of regional tourism. He states that in the Swiss plains, only 3.5 per cent of the land surface is uncultivated, and the shrinking of natural biotypes threatens half the indigenous species of flora and fauna. Some areas have been protected through the creation of reserves and natural parks. But, between sanctuaries and concrete jungle, he believes there are alternative ways to reconcile economic and environmental interests that favour quality over quantity. He suggests that throughout the Alps, common limits should be fixed for development and infrastructure, and that vast areas (particularly the glaciers, which have not yet been exploited) should be left intact.

The Sion Valais in Switzerland is currently bidding for the 2006 Olympic Games. The organizers have the firm desire to reconcile the Games and the environment. No major constructions are planned for short-term use within the sensitive Alpine environment, and priority has been given to the use of existing facilities.

Conservation groups

Conservation groups are a particularly pro-active force throughout Switzerland. For example, providing new lift facilities in Verbier for the increasingly more discerning consumer is not easy. In France, queuing problems are solved as soon as they emerge by developing new lift systems. If Téléverbier (Verbier's powerful lift company), and its director Louis Moix, decide to invest in a new lift, plans must first of all be accepted by the environmental departments within the commune. When an announcement is made to the public about such plans, there are two powerful organizations that can block development. The first is the League Valaisan pour la Protection de Nature (LVPN), and the second is the World Wildlife Fund (WWF). Both Moix and tourist office director Patrick Messeiller disapprove of the latter group's actions, if not its motives: Moix, because the WWF will not sit down at a negotiating table; Messeiller, because if the WWF objects to Verbier's plans the onus is on the resort to conduct and pay for impact studies that the Fund can then use *against* the development. Messeiller believes that in coming years it will be almost impossible to get approval for new lifts unless it is proved that they are absolutely necessary (P. Messeiller, personal communication 1997).

Development and management

In Verbier, environmental issues are starting to play an important part in development plans. François Perraudin, local journalist and president of the Commission de la Zone Protégée – the protected zone of the commune – talks about *développement durable* (sustainable development) and the necessity of finding a balance between the needs of the local economy and the needs of the environment. He believes that communities cannot ignore the economic benefits that lift operators bring to a resort such as Verbier, but that the agriculture and natural resources must be given serious consideration in any impact analysis. He suggests that for all big projects, lift companies employ specialists or consultants, knowledgeable in countryside ecology (F. Perraudin, personal communication 1997). He, and Patrick Messeiller, believe that because half of their 300 square kilometre commune (the largest in Switzerland) is protected, Verbier can claim to be part of an environmentally friendly area. Since the arrival of Louis Moix (arguably Verbier's most powerful decision-maker), there has been evidence of the lift company making changes to protect the environment. For example, under the main Medran lift, slopes have been fenced off to protect delicate shrubs and trees. However, because there is no communication with the public, no messages informing skiers of the reason for the fences, the skiers just duck under the barriers. Even in Meribel, a resort in the French Tarentaise where conservation is less overt, there are signposts indicating nature parks, and notices asking skiers to respect the environment when skiing off-piste.

If Verbier is to make a commitment to reducing air and eye pollution, then long-term plans must be set in place to bring about a reduction in resort traffic. Visitors should be encouraged to use public transport, and this means Verbier should make a move towards being a car-less resort. Eight Swiss mountain communities, including Zermatt and Wengen, have implemented a total ban on vehicular traffic. Of course, the decision is not always spurred by environmental concerns (i.e. confined physical settings), and a resort like Verbier has the infrastructure in place to accommodate thousands of cars whose owners may choose to drive elsewhere if they cannot bring their vehicles. For this reason alone, the tourist office director, Patrick Messeiller, believes a move to ban cars would come up against strong opposition. This is a typical example of commercial and environmental interests in conflict.

Responsible marketing

If Verbier decides to 'green' operations, it will need to market its environmental programmes just as it marketed its new high-speed Funispace lift that cost 27 million francs. (This involved a large promotional campaign at home and overseas.) Most importantly, it must find ways to communicate environmental commitment to visitors, and should publish environmental practices and results in all languages (the pamphlet produced recently by the Swiss transport companies on skiing and nature was published in French and German only).

In recognizing the need to create environmental education programmes as an added attraction or recreational opportunity at the ski area, Téléverbier has introduced a 'Piste Game' for those interested in playing a game that has a bearing on the sustainable development of the area. An illustrated brochure provides various explanations on the subjects of the human and geographical background of the region, flora and fauna, rocks, tourism and mountain agriculture, and includes various questions set out as riddles. Replies to these riddles lead to various points on the piste, where the players will find an amusing game, as well as signs that will pose supplementary questions. Correct answers are put into a draw and winners receive various prizes (including a season's ski pass). The game has been translated from French into German and English.

Responsible operators

Switzerland is still suffering from the perception that it is an expensive destination, and this is tending to limit volume growth at the moment. However, despite a strong currency, and few economies to offer the skier, Switzerland will continue to sell on quality to a certain section of the market, especially advanced skiers who are looking for excellence and variety of snow. If Verbier can improve its quality, which includes adopting the principles of sustainable tourism, then committed skiers will continue to frequent the resort.

As mentioned earlier in this chapter, Alp Action surveyed ski operators who were members of AITO, a group which has always stressed its green credentials, and out of 29 companies, only one had an environmental policy. As yet, there is no evidence to suggest that any of the dozen or so UK operators in Verbier see a niche-marketing opportunity in adopting the principles of responsible tourism. But without their co-operation, the green ski resort will be that much harder to achieve.

Responsible tourists

For most experienced British skiers, Verbier would be in the top five in Europe for the skiing 'experience', and certainly in the top five for expense. It could be argued that because Verbier attracts a more up-market, discerning and educated visitor, such clients will be aware of environmental issues, and will be prepared to pay more for a greener product. However, there is little evidence in Europe to suggest that skiers, especially those in the UK, will pay a higher price for a more environmentally friendly skiing holiday. In the early days of the environmental and ethical 'revolution', astute observers recognized that one of the greatest mistakes any marketer could make would be to confuse what consumers *say* they will pay for with what they will *actually* pay for. Clearly, this is an area that requires further in-depth research. However, Verbier should keep skiers informed about any efforts made to improve the environment, and tourists should be encouraged to play their part. This may involve requesting that guests keep their cars in the valley, educating skiers as to the problems caused by skiing off-piste, and pointing out the environmental and economic costs of dropping litter on the slopes.

The benefits and constraints for Verbier

There is a wide range of potential benefits that greening might bring for a destination such as Verbier (Swarbrooke, 1994). These include:

1. Reductions in the cost base of the destination, through, for example, savings from energy conservation measures;
2. Improving the public reputation of the resort and helping it project a quality image;
3. Allowing the destination to appeal to the more affluent customers, who tend to be the sector of the society more interested in green issues;
4. Enhancing the reputation of the resort with government regulators and peer groups;
5. Giving present and potential investors the impression that the management of the resort is sensitive to changes in consumer behaviour;
6. Making resort staff feel more positive about what they do for a living.

However, Verbier will face both constraints and dangers in greening the resort. Based on Swarbrooke's 'constraints on greening' (1994) barriers include:

1. The paucity of understanding or even interest in green issues that existing customer base may currently have – there is the danger that radical greening may alienate such customers;
2. The willingness to pay of customers who may need to be asked to pay a higher price for a greener product;
3. The initial capital costs of greening;
4. The resort's past behaviour and current reputation that may make it difficult for it to establish a credible reputation as a green destination;
5. The culture of the destination and the attitudes of workers that may not be sympathetic towards the idea of greening.

From the evidence provided in the first half of this chapter, it is clear that the 'greening' of ski resorts is a necessity for sustainable tourism in the mountains. Taking the definitions of sustainable tourism into account, a sustainable ski resort community will be committed to developing only in such ways as will protect and sustain the resort's natural assets for future generations. By staying true to this vision the pioneers of the first 'green ski resort' will become model examples on how to marry economics, recreation and the environment. By developing and applying a model for the greening of ski resorts to the Swiss destination of Verbier, the author has shown that this particular resort has a long way to go before it can claim to be green.

CHAPTER 7

Prospects for the Industry

INTRODUCTION

This chapter looks at the future prospects for the ski industry, based on forecasts, trends and attitudes to winter sports. It considers how technology is likely to have a huge impact on the skiing product and how it is distributed, and makes recommendations for those marketing the skiing product and the destinations that provide winter sports. The author argues for deeper segmentation of both the existing and potential market, and makes some predictions for the future of the ski industry – a future that, although uncertain, offers some exciting prospects.

7.1 MATURITY OR GROWTH?

In North America, and in Europe, as far as one can tell, skiing has actually decreased in popularity. Latest figures from North America (Otten and King 1996) suggest that skiing is still on the decline. In 1994–5, skier visits were down approximately 3.6 per cent, dropping to 52.7 million from 54.6 million. It appears that the number of North American skiers peaked at 12 million in 1988. There are, however, more potential skiers in North America today than there were in the 1970s and 1980s (Otten and King 1996). Otten and King, subjecting the ski industry in North America to the strategic planning technique of 'STEEP' analysis (in which one considers the social, technical, environmental, economic and political aspects of the marketplace), suggest that it is facing several challenges. These include: an aging core market of skiers; a lack of time for skiing due to the rise in two-income families; rising costs in technology required for new lifts and snow-making machines; more and more attractive free-time and disposable-income alternatives in the marketplace; no heroes in ski industry; minimal media coverage for skiing; only 15 per cent of North Americans have the risk-activity orientation and the financial wherewithal to engage in snow sports; the continuing rise in cost of operations (and thus the continuing rise in cost of entry into the sport); the perception of skiing as a sport exclusively for the wealthy (and so class issues arise); and, finally, the possible perception by the potential market that skiing is harmful to the environment.

On the positive side, the following points were made in Otten and King's analysis: there is an appeal to risk sports and a bubble of new potential skiers in the pipeline; there is greater interest in travel – and more economic strength – among minorities; lifts are better and faster, meaning greater comfort and more skiing for the dollar; snow conditions are better than ever, owing to snow-making and grooming; there are better and more effective means of reaching the market than have been traditionally employed (direct mail, Internet, etc.); money is currently comparatively cheap for investments in skiing; and, finally, skiing can be addictive and many families will make it fit into their budget.

Similar challenges face the European and the UK ski industry. At the first UK National Ski Conference in 1993, a Henley Centre report looked at UK leisure trends and the prospects for skiing (Stewart 1993). From this report there appear to be eight main trends that will affect the skiing industry over the next decade. These are:

1. A slow, steady economic growth: the Centre's forecast is for overall GDP growth of 2.1 per cent over the next 5 years, with growth of 2 per cent forecast for consumer spending overall.

2. A more cautious consumer and an emphasis on value for money: consumer confidence is expected to remain subdued owing to concerns about job security, negative equity and an indebted society.

3. To the year 2000, the real incomes of the top 20 per cent of the population will grow by over 30 per cent, while the incomes of those in the bottom 20 per cent will remain broadly static. So, within the overall backdrop of slower, steadier growth, there remain considerable opportunities among the higher-income groups, who have greater discretion and among whom holiday spending will be an important priority.

4. An aging population: there will be a decline in the number of 16–34 year olds (a drop of about 10 per cent), but an increase of 12 per cent in the numbers of 35–44 year olds, and a corresponding increase in the number of children. Also, there will be an 11 per cent increase in the size of the middle-aged population of 45–59 year olds. There will therefore have to be greater emphasis focused on families and those in the post-family, middle-aged groups over the next decade.

5. A continued fragmentation in household structure: the main point of interest is that the fastest growing household type is the 35–59-year-old, single-person household. This suggests an important potential niche market for older single people.

6. A growth in second holidays and short breaks: this will come about because of more flexible working patterns, more free time, greater annual holiday entitlement and an increase in leisure spending. Given the overall importance attached to holidays (it ranks behind only washing machines and cars as a priority for expenditure), the holiday market is expected to be one of the major beneficiaries of the growth in leisure spending forecast to the year 2000.

7. A greater focus on activities and a more adventurous tourist: this is partly the result of the majority being engaged in more sedentary occupations, as well as the impact of increasing health consciousness. Also, the more travel people undertake, the more they want to do. They also tend to become more adventurous and confident as their level of affluence and travel experience increases, and seek greater independence and flexibility.

8. A rise in concern about safety and the environment: there are worries that skiing is not environmentally friendly, and this is a challenge that the industry must confront. Also, despite the increase in activity holidays, people are still worried about the safety of certain sports, and skiing is still perceived as unsafe.

Table 7.1 Market size (and forecasts) from Mintel and Crystal. *Source*: Mintel (1994, 1996) and Crystal Holidays Industry Reports (1996, 1997).

Year	Holidays (000s)	
	Crystal	Mintel
1988–9	–	710
1989–90	–	675
1990–1	–	610
1991–2	–	635
1992–3	730	616
1993–4	747	635
1994–5	730	625
1995–6	760	645
1996–7	830	630 (estimate)
1997–8	–	640 (estimate)
1998–9	–	646 (estimate)
1999–2000	–	663 (estimate)

The UK ski market appears to have now reached maturity; this means that although it will continue to form a significant part of winter holiday sales, it will grow at a much reduced rate. Lewis and Wild (1995) predict that the average rate of growth over the next five years will be approximately 5 per cent per annum. This forecast is in line with that of Mintel's, who in 1996 used the Statgraphics Time Series package to forecast the market to 2000. However, their forecast is well below the figures provided by Crystal Holidays in their industry reports of the last two years. Understandably, these are quite bullish, but they are the only statistics available at this time. Figures provided by Mintel and Crystal are compared in Table 7.1. Some segments of the market will grow at a much higher rate. It is estimated that independent ski holidays will increase twice as quickly as the general market (Lewis and Wild 1995). The opening of the channel tunnel and improvements in European motorways now allow easy travel to within the last few miles of major resorts in France, Switzerland and Austria. Also, tour operators are coming up with some innovative new products to cater for the growing segments. These include dedicated programmes for beginners, comprehensive arrangements for families, clinics for advanced skiers, and the emergence of the all-inclusive holiday.

7.2 ATTITUDES TOWARDS SKIING

Current attitudes dictate our perception of the future, a future which did not looked encouraging for the skiing industry in the early 1990s. Economic recession, increasing media reports of accidents, global warming and the environmental lobby all took their toll on public perception. The industry shuddered in 1994 when Britain's largest tour operator, Thomson, drastically curtailed its destination offerings, following remarks from its chief executive, Charles Newbold, that skiing was fading from fashion. However, the following year Thomson reinforced its commitment to the ski business with a revamped programme and brochure, reintroduced US destinations and increased offerings to the Alps. With the acquisition of Crystal in 1998, Thomson has emerged as the major player in the skiing market.

According to most city analysts, however, the recession is over for the moment (although a new one could be just around the corner), and global warming is a phenomenon an increasing number of scientists doubts exists at all. The last two years have seen excellent snow falls in the USA and Europe. Accidents will, unfortunately, always occur and be reported, but the Alps are becoming as safe as North America, and many UK operators distribute the Fédération Internationale de Ski (FIS) Skiers' Code to their customers.

Environmental awareness, however perceived, will have the greatest impact on skiing in our lifetimes, especially in the Alps (Sager 1996). The environmental lobby has lowered its voice, partly because so many of its demands have been met. The most extreme environmentalist would ban skiing altogether. The more moderate is content with the achievement of banning helicopter skiing, off-piste skiing in the woods and new lift construction. In the Alps, the only new lifts for the foreseeable future will be replacements for existing installations. One possible answer to ecological concern is to put ski-lifts underground: Saas Fee, Zermatt, Val d'Isere, Tignes and Les Deux Alpes already have underground funiculars. By adopting sound environmental policies, ski resorts, by responding to public concerns, can gain a competitive advantage by marketing their destinations as 'green' (Hudson 1996). The Austrian village of Lech sets an example for the future with its policy of limiting the maximum number of skiers on any day to 14,000.

7.3 THE IMPACT OF TECHNOLOGY

In the near future, the trend in ski-lifts is towards large, stand-up *télécabines* running at twice the speed of normal lifts. High-speed chair-lifts, in existence throughout North America, have yet to appear in large numbers in the Alps. Last year, the world's first centrally heated ski-lift was opened at the US resort of Killington, Vermont. Costing £12 million, skiers in its eight-seat gondola cabins are warmed by hot air from underfloor heaters that keep the temperature at 50 degrees. Four 'VIP' cabins, costing $20 extra per ride, have reclining seats, carpets, drinks-holders and audio-cassette players. And, if skiers grow hungry in Sweden and do not want to remove their skis, there is the world's first ski-through McDonalds! The McSki opened in 1996 at the resort of Lindvallen, 260 miles north of Stockholm. Skiers simply pull in to a window, as in a drive-through restaurant, make their order, and then take their meal to seats outside.

In the USA, where a culture of people addicted to information has been created, several new projects are under consideration (Freedman 1992). Touch-screen terminals at various sites around the mountain will in the future provide detailed, graphically displayed information on everything from slope conditions to the facilities at different types of accommodation. Automated room reservation systems will take information from callers via touch-tone phone or, possibly, voice recognition. Artificial intelligence systems will assist with some of the snow-making and staffing decision-making. Some resort operators (in Killington, for example) have issued 'frequent skier' cards that can be barcode-scanned at the ticket window to track and reward repeat business. As a bonus, this type of service will provide more information than ever on the resort's best customers.

With equipment, technology is tending towards the futurist, with designs for computerized bindings already in the pipeline, and future improvements in materials guaranteed to bring even closer the ideal marriage between comfort and performance in skis and boots. Some confidence in the future of skiing stems from the next generation of skis that have recently entered the market (Petrick 1996).

Several marketing buzz words have been used to describe them, including parabolics, super sidecuts, hourglass, deep dish, and shaped skis. Shaped skis – the generic term most often used to describe these new designs – make everyone a better skier, regardless of ability level, right from the very first run. Both the operational and marketing implications of this are profound. The shaped skis allow even intermediate skiers to execute tightly controlled turns with minimum effort. Snowboarders can tackle powder within a week. Most recreational skiers never will unless, of course, they try the new wide skis, 'Fat Boys', which have brought powder skiing within the reach of most intermediate skiers. These innovations change the range and ability levels of all recreational skiers. Suddenly the most challenging terrain becomes accessible.

Anyone who learned to ski on wood wearing leather boots can appreciate the revolution in space-age material and ski design that has allowed the ordinary person to ski better today than Olympic athletes of only a few decades ago. Similar advances in lightweight, waterproof, breathable fabrics have vastly increased creature comfort. Improvements in both fields are sure to continue. Driven by the desire for success in downhill racing, the skis, the waxes, and even the clothing, are fiercely tested. The buzz word in ski technology at the moment is titanium. After the huge success of titanium golf-clubs and tennis racquets, designers have begun adding this extremely expensive, lightweight element to skis.

Technology has also changed the relative incidence of skiing injuries over the last 30 years. The relationships between skier, boot, binding, ski and snow have changed greatly. The ski equipment and techniques of the 1950s did not permit rapid directional change, resulting in a high incidence of ankle fractures. The introduction of the higher, stiffer, ankle-retention boot and firm, cambered composite skis in the 1960s helped reduce ankle injuries, but caused an increase in knee ligament injuries, particularly to the anterior cruciate ligament (ACL). The ACL is injured in 45 per cent of knee injuries and accounts for 10–20 per cent of all skiing injuries (Chissel, Feagin, Warme, Lambert, King and Johnson 1996). However, ski injury rates decreased from about 5–8 per 1000 skiers/days in the 1950s to about 2–3 per 1000 skiers/days in the early 1980s and have remained fairly constant since. Beginners are between three and five times as likely to be injured as advanced skiers.

Snowboarders, on the other hand, are twice as likely to be injured than skiers. Most snowboarders wear soft-shell boots, with a rubber sole anchored to the board with non-releasable bindings. This type of boot allows considerable motion of the ankle joint to aid turning, but risks injury to the ankle. Unlike the high incidence of knee injuries in skiers, ankle and upper limb injuries are more common in snowboarders. The injury rate of snowboarders is about 6–10 per 1000 boarders/days and the injuries are mainly sustained by beginners. About 60 per cent of all injuries occur to snowboarders with fewer than twenty days experience. By contrast, only 34 per cent of skiing injuries are sustained by beginners.

Changes in technology are also likely to influence the way skiing holidays are purchased. The Internet – specifically the easy-to-use world wide web implementation of the Internet – offers a tremendous opportunity for ski operators and ski resorts to adopt closely targeted marketing. Potential customers, using software called a Web browser installed on a home computer, can dial up the operator's brochure and reservation information, or, alternatively, request weather or accommodation details from the resort. Having obtained this information, the technology is now available for customers to reserve and pay for a ski package. Virgin have introduced the first-ever 'Ski-D Rom', and websites now transmit live pictures from the ski slopes, so that skiers can see snow conditions in the resort of their choice. The ability to do this on the world wide web indicates the enormous potential of this global information highway, which is affecting all aspects of life, including travel and tourism. In fact, you can – if you know how – take a video-run on a downhill course, shop for clothing and equipment, and check out resort and snow reports anywhere in the world. It is possible to browse through ski magazines, buy cheap flights, rent chalets (having first 'looked' at the bedrooms), and chat live and exchange information with other skiers and snowboarders anywhere in the world.

One of the biggest challenges facing ski resorts is getting inside the head of the guest to gather information vital to marketing and budget decisions (Newhart 1997). On-site, intercept-and-quiz chair-lift surveys can be intrusive, and the results are questionable (dependent on how rigorously the survey is controlled). Silver Mountain, Idaho uses a new point-of-view (POV) system. It consists of a small metal box with a keypad that allows guests to answer area-specific survey questions privately at their own pace. Using such a system, ski resorts can fulfil their research objectives: the vendor can even design and analyse a customized survey for each particular resort.

7.4 SEGMENTING THE SKIING MARKET OF THE FUTURE

In the past, too much emphasis has been placed on marketing to current skiers. The author recommends, however, that the skiing market be segmented into existing skiers and potential non-skiers.

Marketing to non-skiers

Research has shown that many of the constraints affecting the sport of skiing are based on intra-personal misconceptions (Hudson 1998a; Williams and Basford

1992). Somehow, these perceptions and attitudes must be changed. Even if the industry could agree on a targeted national advertising campaign, what should the message be? Currently, communication is predominantly directed to the converted, with too narrow a focus on those that visit ski resorts or read the few skiing publications. If the sport is to be revitalized, then the audience cannot be only skiers. In North America, efforts have been made to tap into the 35 million whose demographic profiles make them potential skiers. However, for many reasons – insufficient funding, flawed research, complications of merger, recession, poor staffing – the efforts have been unsuccessful.

Can one alter travel behaviour by altering the factors that seem to influence it? Kotler (1982) suggests that in order to change attitudes, marketers can:

1. modify the characteristics of the tourist product (real positioning);
2. alter beliefs about the product (psychological positioning);
3. alter beliefs about competitive products (competitive depositioning);
4. change the relevant weights of the product attributes;
5. induce attention to certain attributes;
6. modify the tourist's ideal levels for certain attributes.

For the non-skier, changing preconceived attitudes requires education. Education has been cited as one of the most powerful influences over travel behaviour (Zimmer, Brayley and Searle 1995), and this includes information through advertising. It may not be possible to overcome one's fear of heights, lack of desire for physical challenge, or apprehension at learning a new sport. However, it is clear that the decision to ski or not is income-sensitive; creative marketers can influence travel behaviour by increasing the perceived income of the market or by reducing its influence through establishment of a sense of value and purchasing power in the minds of potential consumers. It is also clear that non-skiers perceive skiing to be dangerous, and so marketing messages must counter this argument.

The value of skiing is centred around the excitement that it generates, but the ski industry appears to have a problem marketing this excitement. Products outside the industry can often be successfully associated with the sport in order to generate this excitement. One example is a recent venture by Disney: when Disney was seeking to project the image of something exciting, risky and dangerous, it chose skiing. One of its attractions in Florida, called Blizzard Beach, has summits, snow, peaks, a warming hut and a chair-lift – all in tribute to excitement (Nelson 1995a). Since Blizzard Beach opened in April 1995, its capacity of 5000 has, according to the public relations people, been met every day. The daily fees are about $25 per adult and $20 for children. The featured attractions emanate from a 120-foot-high 'mountain' that has toboggan slides, flumes, inner-tube chutes and a simulated ski-jump called the Summit Plummet. The developers believe that people want to be in a kind of ski resort atmosphere where there is a perception of thrills and chills.

The question for the marketer is how to *re*capture the essence of skiing – the exhilaration, fascination, sense of independence and freedom, beauty of the mountains, rush of adrenaline, sore muscles, and the incredible high that skiers feel at the end of days of skiing. The consumer passion and emotional commitment that accounted for skiing's tremendous popularity and growth since World War II needs to be regenerated. Somehow, ski marketers need to recapture the magic, and think creatively to put this magic into images and language that the information age demands.

According to Csikszentmihalyi (1975), professor and former chair of the Department of Psychology at the University of Chicago, most people in contemporary society suffer either anxiety or boredom. What they are missing between these two polls is the satisfaction and happiness that comes from activities that provide both complexity and challenge. This state of mind he terms 'flow', which is achieved when a person is involved in something for the sake of the goal itself. The rewards in facing a challenge like skiing, at whatever level, says Csikszentmihalyi, are what allow people to fulfil their individuality. According to Nelson (1996), skiing offers an ideal opportunity to experience flow. Perhaps the industry is missing a chance to send a 'flow' message to potential recruits. Currently, the message used to sell skiing is that it is 'fun', but what exactly is fun? Fun for one person might be dramatically different from what is fun for another.

Messages sent out to non-participants could be two-sided in order to incorporate these theories about the sport. Rather than playing down the expense of the sport, which has been shown to be the major constraint perceived by non-skiers, one should state that it *is* an expensive activity, but one that brings emotional well-being that is worth the cost. Furthermore, the messages used today downplay the risks but do not mention the psychic rewards, mention the discomforts without stressing the energizing invigoration, note the difficulty of learning without emphasizing the sense of achievement in developing skills. Foxhall and Goldsmith (1994) refer to conclusive evidence that, within a specified context, two-sided appeals may be more effective than one-sided appeals (Faison 1961; Hovland, Janis and Kelley 1948). The authors recommend that the market or segment receiving the message must be currently unconvinced about the product's attractiveness, and conclude that those most persuaded by the two-sided appeal tend to be highly educated. This would suggest that non-skiers would be prime targets for a two-sided message.

Consumer interest in skiing can be greatly stimulated by media coverage of skiing events, such as the Winter Olympics in 1992 and 1996. In addition, the BBC's *Ski Sunday* has proved popular (with weekly viewing figures of 3 million), as has specialist and national press coverage of the sport. As mentioned in Chapter 4, Mintel (1994) reported that television is the preferred medium for skiing as it lends itself more to the excitement and action-based nature of the sport, and 16.6 per cent of consumers claimed to watch skiing on television, whereas only 1.5 per cent actually ski, so television could be instrumental in sending out the correct messages about the sport to potential participants, thereby helping to overcome their intra-personal constraints.

There are many who believe that there is a direct correlation between the images and superstars that are created on television and the desire of the sports fan to participate (Leiweke 1996). Leiweke argues that skiing has done a very poor job of showcasing the sport on television, even though for fourteen days every four years much of the country has watched it as its second favourite Olympic activity. Figure skating, by contrast, has done an excellent job of programming its sport and creating stars. The sport has built a very large television audience, and at grass-roots level there is a whole new level of interest and participation in figure skating. As the new head of US Skiing (USS), Leiweke's job is to design and sell good programming for skiing in the US; develop stars, sponsor partnerships and packages; and work out co-ordinated merchandising and promotional programmes. His answer is to create made-for-television events that would present competition that the American sports fan likes and which he or she would watch.

Skiing is not a mass appeal sport, but the ski industry in the UK may wish to monitor US efforts to manipulate the media. Somehow, the favourable images of skiing must be presented to a wary audience of British non-participants, in a manner that overcomes the obstacles that keep them away from the sport. One of these obstacles is the perception that it is dangerous (Hudson 1998a; Williams and Basford 1992). However, Dr Michael Turner, chief medical advisor to the British Ski and Snowboard Federation, has compiled statistics on relative risks, that blow a hole in everybody's assumptions (Bosely 1998) (see Figure 7.1). Top of the dangerous sports list comes rugby, with an injury rate of 95.7 per 1000 participant days. Skiing notches up just 2.6 per 1000 participant days, which is around the same as table tennis. The perception of danger possibly comes from the fact that skiers see the injured on the ski slopes because thousands of skiers are heading down the mountain at the same time. If the slopes were covered with the same number of injured rugby players, the carnage would be very visible.

Figure 7.1 Skiing is not as dangerous as many other sports.

Marketing to skiers

In terms of promotion, many of the ideas suggested above can be implemented for both skiers and non-skiers. Many studies (Hudson 1998a; Mintel 1996; Williams and Dossa 1995), have found financial constraints to be the major obstacles keeping existing skiers from further participation. So, as already mentioned, promotion should state that skiing *is* an expensive activity, but it brings emotional well-being worth the cost. Skiers are also significantly more concerned about the lack of snow and about overcrowded ski slopes than are non-skiers. Suggestions as to how the industry can counteract these constraints follow later in this chapter.

Those who have experienced the positive aspects of skiing (the exhilaration, beauty of the mountains, rush of adrenaline, etc.) require constant reminders of these emotional benefits. In the UK, 3.75 million people have skied in the last five years, but Mintel (1996) suggests that there are only 1.5 million active skiers, and, of these, less than half ski every year. The drop-out rate for skiing is high – higher than for most popular sports (Jackson and Dunn 1988) – and more effort is needed to keep participants interested. As already emphasized, media coverage of skiing events is important in this respect.

Further segmentation of the market

The potential ski market (non-skiers and latent demand) can be segmented further into five major groups, each of which will require different marketing messages. These are: the aging market, families, teenagers, the long-haul market, and women.

The aging market

The declining numbers of young adults will have an adverse affect on the market, and destinations and operators will need to broaden the appeal of skiing to those aged 35–59, a group that is increasing in size. In the USA the numbers of skiers over 55 years old has increased since 1987 by 40 per cent, and half of these skiers did not learn to ski until they were 36 or older (Witchel 1989). According to Spring (1995a), skiers over 50 years old tend to be male, live active lives, be knowledgeable about health and fitness, and, frequently, have schedules flexible enough to enable them to ski in low season. In the UK there has also been a gradual drifting of the age profiles of skiers, such that there are now higher proportions of skiers in the 35–60 age group (Lewis and Wild 1995). Mintel (1996) and Hudson (1998b) have also suggested that the skiing population is getting older.

While ensuring that young people acquire the skiing habit will continue to be important, it is imperative that the industry reorients its offer to cater to the needs of families and older age groups. The demographic trends are exacerbated by income trends, and those with the highest amount of income are in the family and middle-age groups. The middle-age group will become an increasing focus across a range of consumer markets. It should be remembered that those entering middle age in the 1990s were the youth of the 1960s. They tend to be much more experienced and adventurous consumers.

This middle-age group has very high levels of discretion owing to the convergence of a number of factors. Members of this group are at the peak of their earnings' potential, their children are flying the nest, and they are the 'inheritor' generation. Their parents were really the first generation of owner-occupiers and, as they die, they leave fairly substantial bequests to their middle-aged offspring. Many in this group are no longer in the habit of participating in a range of activities that they may have given up when they had children and so they need to be wooed back.

Marketing skiing to this age group is not easy. First of all, how does one address this market segment? Despite the proliferation of magazines and television shows aimed at, or featuring, old men and women, in our society, age is an anathema. In the US, 'senior', with its connotations of status and seasoning, seems to be emerging as the euphemism of choice. The European ski industry may wish to adopt some of the US ideas that attract this age group to the mountains. In Aspen, Colorado, a 'Fit Over 50' programme offers a series of seminars plus a ski package aimed at developing a life-plan for the years beyond 50. Co-ordinated with the Aspen ski school, skiing is the focal point of a series of week-long seminars that aim to teach controlled risk, stress management, and gaining and maintaining health and fitness. As many as 30 people are enrolled in each of three sessions, which cost up to $1400 (including lifts, lessons, room, breakfasts, parties and final banquet). What the US operators have found, is that seniors seem to look first for fun and an opportunity for congenial companionship; next, for an environment in which they feel confident; and last, for an opportunity to improve. Ski operators and destinations in Europe that are planning for the 50-plus tidal wave of the next decade may wish to keep those preferences in mind.

Families

Mintel (1996) has shown that the transition to family stage in the life-cycle makes a big difference to skiing frequency, with the proportion of frequent skiers immediately falling from 11 per cent to 2 per cent. Similarly, Williams and Dossa

Figure 7.2 Mainstream operators will have to cater for the growing family segment.

(1995) found that, for women, having children was the biggest reason for dropping out of the sport, and that for men, family commitments were the second biggest constraint behind financial factors. For both sexes, the main reason for returning to the sport was because the children were old enough to ski. An aging population indicates that there will be more and more families entering the market – to the year 2000, there will be an increase of 12 per cent in the numbers of 35–44 year olds (Stewart 1993) – and there will therefore have to be a greater marketing emphasis towards families. Statistics from A. C. Nielsen (see Table 7.2) indicate that the number of families taking ski trips is growing, and this segment now accounts for 25.1 per cent of the total ski-package market. There are several small, specialist operators who cater specifically for the family market, but mainstream operators – and destinations – will have to start catering for this particular growing market segment (Figure 7.2).

Table 7.2 Skiing holidays with children, 1994/5 to 1997/8. *Source*: A. C. Nielsen (1998).

Date	Package skiing holidays with children	Percentage of package market
1994–5	62 413	22.5
1995–6	70 021	24.7
1996–7	77 850	24.3
1997–8	88 880	25.1

Teenagers

This is a critical group for the ski industry. Continuity theory (Atchley 1989) suggests that as individuals age, they tend to sustain consistent patterns of behaviour and are not prone to major shifts in likes, dislikes and general activities. This theory of leisure behaviour suggests that the largest potential impact on travel behaviour comes at a relatively early age.

Despite the decline in young adults, the sport is still dominated by the younger age group, with over a quarter of the market still in the fifteen to nineteen years age group. With changes in the local financial management of British schools, and changes in the rules governing the supervision of outdoor activities in British schools, there has been a decline in the number of school trips being organized through Local Education Authorities. Concern has been expressed that this is going to have an adverse effect on the recruitment of young people into the market (Mintel 1994). However, there are trends that counter this argument. There is a growing number of operators offering family holidays, and it may be that recruitment in the young will now be increasingly via this route, combined with a growing interest in snowboarding. The snowboard boom, which has had a greater impact on young people, has caused the ski industry to assess its effect on the market, and many operators and destinations are now catering for this growing market segment.

However, in order to successfully market to this group, the ski industry needs to understand it more fully. Experts say that teenagers take lessons to meet other teenagers, ski/snowboard at high speed, explore the mountain with like-minded companions, and, only incidentally, improve ski/snowboard technique (Rand 1996). The US has learned that the keys to attracting this age group (and, if the kids come, so do their parents) are good leadership, complete separation from younger kids, and space.

For the European ski industry, marketing will be central to the ability of operators and ski resorts to attract teenagers. Advertising and promotional literature that is directed specifically at teenagers and that itemizes the benefits, flexibility and 'cool' aspects of the offerings may be the way to cultivate this group. Teenagers may be impossible to please and difficult to understand, but they are important customers with considerable clout – both now and in the future.

Long-haul market

Much more could be done by Europe's ski industry to tap long-haul markets. This could be particularly promising in the latter weeks or months of the traditional winter season, so that Americans or Japanese, say, could combine a few days skiing with tours of European cities and other attractions in the spring.

Cockerell (1994) has identified a potential market of four million Americans interested in skiing in Europe: this is almost ten times higher than the actual share of Americans who have skied in Europe in the past. There are other emerging long-haul markets that could generate steady growth for Europe through the remainder of the decade and beyond: these include South Africa, Australia, Mexico, Argentina and Brazil. The biggest growth market for western ski resorts is Japan. According to *Maison de la France* (see Cockerell 1994) international winter sports business from Japan rose by an amazing 90 per cent in 1992–3.

Exploring potential new and emerging markets can, however, often be expensive, difficult to target and hard to predict. European resorts have had mixed results in attempting to attract the Japanese. It is the Americans, through their attention to detail and investment in market research, who have had the most success in marketing to ethnic groups. The resort of Northstar in California, for example, has been successful in tapping the Asian-American market. It discovered from research that the average Asian-American is younger, better educated and has a higher income than the average American. The family is particularly important: it enjoys doing activities as an extended family group. Asian-Americans are extremely loyal to brands, and there is a higher comfort level with technology than for the general population.

If European operators and ski resorts are marketing to distinct cultural and ethnic markets, they should be alert to cultural differences, both those that may present problems for the staff to work through, and those that represent opportunities to be enhanced. For example, Verbier in Switzerland has experienced problems in offering ski school services to the Japanese (Hudson 1998b). Differences have showed up in how the Europeans teach skiing and snowboarding, and in the manner in which students are complimented or praised. For instance, the Japanese seem very willing to take the entry level lessons two or three times, but tend not to take lessons beyond that. In lessons they are much more into practising and perfecting the skill than is the mainstream market. They like the controlled environment of a ski school teaching area – more so than the mainstream customers – and seem to have a higher fear factor. For these and other reasons, internal employee education should be an important part of any campaign to attract particular cultures or nationalities. Some resorts, like Zermatt in Switzerland, have chosen to overcome many barriers by employing a large percentage of Japanese staff. Maurer (1996) believes that the Asian market is a complex one, but one that is inexpensive and relatively easy in terms of identifying the appropriate vehicles for reaching it. Capturing such a market requires a long-term, ongoing effort on the part of Europe's ski industry, but once it is captured, it is likely to remain loyal to the product.

Women

The life-cycle framework for explaining patterns in leisure constraints and negotiation strategies has been augmented by the inclusion of gender as a mediating variable (Jackson and Henderson 1995; Scott and Jackson 1996). Research has indicated that females are more constrained than males in their leisure behaviour. Raymore *et al.* (1994) and Alexandris and Carrol (1997) have suggested that females perceive intra-personal constraints – such as shyness, self-consciousness, lack of skills and knowledge of the availability of opportunities to participate – more intensely. These results were further supported by Jackson and Henderson (1995). They found that females scored more highly, in the dimensions of social isolation and lack of skills, dimensions that can be categorized as inter-personal and intra-personal constraints respectively. In contrast, males were not found to score more highly than females in any of the constraint dimensions, thereby supporting the findings of Alexandris and Carrol (1997).

Skiing in the UK market is still male-dominated, but is, according to Lewis and Wild (1995), becoming increasingly popular with well-off females. In their surveys they found that in 1985 the ratio of men to women skiers was 1.6 : 1, and that by 1992 this ratio had dropped to 1.3 : 1. However, Mintel (1994) suggests that the percentage of women dropping out of the sport is far more than for men, and that the ratio of men to women was almost 1 : 1 in 1989 compared to 1.5 : 1 in 1993. This would parallel trends in the USA, where women are dropping out of skiing at a worrisome rate (Witchel 1996).

Much of the decline in numbers can be attributed to poor promotion of the benefits and services that skiing can provide for women. Skiing is a male-dominated sport that sends male messages that tend not to receive a positive reaction from women. Hudson (1998c) confirmed that women are significantly more likely to be constrained by intra-personal factors, such as perceived self-skill and the perception of danger. There is also the general 'hassle and fatigue' of skiing, that many of today's working women cannot, and do not, wish to cope with.

A major constraint to potential male skiers is the fact that their partner frequently does not wish to participate; men are significantly more constrained by this factor than women (Hudson 1998c). It is therefore important that the industry targets women specifically. Not only will they then encourage their partner to ski, but they may also influence their children if they have them. Many operators and ski resorts have the services that women require, but they do not promote them adequately or target them specifically enough to women.

According to a 1995 survey from Louis Harris and Associates (Witchel 1996), time is more important than money for women in the demographic groups that are likely to ski. Jackson Hole in the USA is trying to relieve the time pressure by providing a 'seamless, one-call-does-it-all' package that includes not only accommodation, lifts, child care, rental equipment and airport transportation, but dinner reservations and booking reservations for non-skiing activities.

In Europe, in order to bring women skiers – and their families – back to the ski slopes, hard research is required in order to discover why they have dropped out and what will commit them to the sport. What *is* known, confirmed by the Harris survey (Witchel 1996), is that women are more interested in quality than quantity, that they like learning and that they give high priority to supporting others. Resorts should show women that they really care by catering to their concerns. They should consider the following: offering flexible lift tickets (with the option of two or three hours skiing as opposed to a whole day); holding ski school classes with an emphasis on experience, not achievement; and making child care a loss leader. However independent and adventurous a woman may be, studies confirm that her children are still number one priority.

If operators and destinations really want women to come back to skiing, they should have little trouble organizing a hassle-free ski package incorporating some of the ideas above. Many have been refining these services for years. Now they need to be promoted.

7.5 DESTINATION MARKETING OF THE FUTURE

The ski slopes

Most ski destinations must satisfy an increasingly fragmentary and demanding marketplace with more specialized facilities and services, and at the same time assimilate those customer segments so that they share the limited number of ski slopes. As mentioned previously, demographic fragmentation is increasing the number of older customers and creating more families; simultaneously, the youth market is taking to snowboarding, which is a new and special segment in itself. If one adds to this mix the higher demands, new values and tastes, and changes in lifestyle, leisure time and finances of each of these segments, then resorts and operators will have to be even more flexible and diverse in their services. Most ski resorts will have to assimilate these groups on the mountain, creating an atmosphere where none is alienated or made uncomfortable by the presence of others.

Resorts in the United States are investing in 'learning parks' for snowboarders (Olcott 1996) and 'zone-flow systems' for skiers (Isham 1996). For example, at Taos Ski Valley in New Mexico, the beginners' teaching hill is divided into four zones for teaching specific skills. Zone one is the meeting place where classes are divided; zone two is for explaining equipment and teaching walking, balance and stance skills; zone three is to practise balance while moving on skis; and zone four is for learning sidestepping and turns. The slope is reshaped to suit the teaching activities, and after first-time skiers are grouped in the staging zone, instructors take their classes through the four task-specific teaching zones. Just through simple zoning, the resort has seen an increase in the number of beginners returning to ski school for the second day, improving an aspect of the business that has been extremely difficult to penetrate.

Destinations and operators will need to keep monitoring the mix of 'downhillers', the term used in North America to include skiers and snowboarders (Spring 1997). The mix of pure skiers, pure boarders and cross-overs on the slopes of North America showed a dramatic change in the 1996–7 season. Slightly over one in four adult downhillers claimed to be snowboarders, a huge increase from the 16 per cent in 1995–6. Approximately 60 per cent of all snowboarders have skied before, and often practise both sports. Another 35 per cent of cross-overs say they will not ski again, and, of these, over half are over 25, more than two-thirds male and 73 per cent are single. Of the skiing population who have not snowboarded, 31 per cent say they will try it in the next few years. So it is evident that the majority of snowboarders are coming from the ranks of skiers and that the cross-over trend will continue, not just in North America, for the next few years. What is not clear is whether or not snowboarding is a trophy sport for skiers – an attempt to be fashionable – and how many of these cross-overs will stick with boarding to the exclusion of skiing. The data indicates that the core market of downhillers is declining, and the industry should be aware of this. Spring (1997) suggests that it should not matter to ski resorts and operators whether participants see themselves as snowboarders or skiers, just as long as they buy holidays and purchase lift tickets.

In Europe, however, dedicated snowboard brochures have not been successful, and operators should be seeking to send consumers to the resorts that accommodate both groups of downhillers. They will also have to be more flexible in their product offerings, following the example of companies like Panorama. Panorama has taken a lead by introducing the concept of 'switch packs', allowing skiers and snowboarders to switch between equipment for the different sports for a modest fee. A separate challenge for the industry will be to convert boarders who have not skied before into skiers. This will be necessary if snowboarding is just a short-term phenomenon, or if it is found that the physical aspects of snowboarding are suited only to the younger generation.

For existing skiers, one of the main constraints to participation is the problem of overcrowding (Carmichael 1992; Hudson 1998a). The industry analysis in Chapter 2 suggested that the industry was mature and that skiers are skiing fewer hours each day. This, coupled with the rapid increase in alternative activities in the Alps during the winter, could alleviate some of the crowd problems. One area into which ski resorts in the US have invested time and money is lift queues. Ski-lift queues remain (with the exception of accidents) the biggest obstacle to the enjoyment of skiing (Scott 1994). Definitions of precisely what constitutes a queue vary enormously between continents. For Patrick Messeiller, the tourist office director in Verbier – a resort that enjoys a reputation for some of the longest queues in Europe – a skier is not technically in a queue until he or she has been waiting in line for at least twenty minutes (Hudson and Shephard 1998). But for Tom Kelly, director of skiing at Squaw Valley, California, a skier who has had to wait in line for just ten minutes has been so inconvenienced that he or she is entitled to have the cost of that day's skiing refunded (Scott 1994).

Many European ski resorts, especially Verbier, do not offer the same quality of service from their ski-lifts as do their American competitors (Hudson and Shephard

1998). The above example encapsulates the different attitudes to queues on opposite sides of the Atlantic. In the US, lift lines (never 'queues') are an evil that should ideally be avoided at all costs. To this end, US ski resort operators employ far more lift-operating staff than do their European counterparts. They are well trained, approach their job in a professional manner, and offer service with a smile (and occasionally a cup of coffee).

Several seasons of poor snow cover on both sides of the Atlantic had a crippling effect on the ski industry during the late 1980s and early 1990s. Despite the huge investments resorts have made in snow-making equipment, and some relatively good snow conditions over the past few years, 'lack of snow' is still a major constraint to skiing participation, especially for those who have skied before.

One of the first US resorts to invest in snow-making technology was Killington, Vermont. A Boston company named Larchmont introduced snow-making equipment in the early 1960s, and Killington was one of the first resorts in the world to set out Larchmont 'guns' that sprayed out a fine mist of water and air that instantly formed snow-like ice crystals. During the 1960s and 1970s Killington aggressively marketed itself as the ski resort that could be counted on for snow. By overcoming the vagaries of the weather, staying ahead of the technology and then communicating this fact to the public, Killington has remained profitable while others have failed (Freedman 1992). At present, there is no one ski resort in Europe that is renowned for its 'guaranteed' snow. If destinations are going to invest in snow-making, then a budget needs to be set aside to communicate this investment and its benefits to consumers. Of course, not all ski resorts can afford to invest in the machinery, and those resorts that suffer more often from poor snow conditions are often the smaller, lower resorts. To counter this problem, many resorts in the Alps (in France and Italy in particular) have joined their skiing areas and their ski-lifts by the crests that separate them. For example, Vars and Risoul in France have just been unified, and a common ski pass enables the skier to use 54 ski-lifts. As a matter of survival, this trend is likely to continue, as long as environmentalists allow the building of new interlinking lifts.

Another US idea that could be imported to Europe is that of the Family Snowmaking Learning Centre, pioneered by Smugglers Notch, Vermont (Rowan, 1997). The learning centre is literally a ski-through educational experience in which the front side of a pump house is fitted with windows, allowing guests a peek into the inner workings of snow-making. In addition to the pump house, interpretative displays have been set up for guests on weather, snow crystals, effects on the environment and the history of snow-making. The ski school also has made use of the centre, bringing people through and allowing them to play with a computer-simulated snow-making system located inside the building.

Provision of alternative winter sports

It was suggested in Chapter 1 that ski destinations cannot afford to ignore the active non-skier who still travels to the mountains in the winter. Williams and Dossa (1990) estimate that between 20 and 30 per cent of visitors to ski centres in Canada do not ski. An analysis of market trends in Europe suggests that, similarly, an increasing proportion of those who take winter sports holidays on a regular basis do not ski at all. The respective share among the French, for example, is estimated to be as high as 40 per cent (Cockerell 1994). Wickers (1994) suggests that one in eight visitors to Zermatt, one of Switzerland's top ski resorts, does not ski.

Successful resorts of the future will have to treat skiing and snowboarding as forms of entertainment and establish more off-slope diversions. With people spending less and less time on the slopes – an average of three hours a day – resorts need to concentrate more on *après-ski* activities, and not just on shopping and dining. Vail's Adventure ridge, a night-time cornucopia of tubing, sledding and other non-skiing winter escapes, was described on pages 12–13 and has established the appeal of mountain theme parks. Also, the continued demand among baby-boomers for scarce mountain real estate means that boomers at or near retirement age are more likely to pursue leisure activities that are less rigorous than skiing. Active non-skiers will be seeking an increasing number of substitute sports facilities, such as heated swimming pools, mini-gyms, tennis halls, skating rinks and saunas and solaria.

Many ski brochures now provide detailed information about facilities such as tennis halls, snow rafting, skating rinks, horse riding, go-karting, tobogganing, curling and hot-air ballooning, that individual resorts may offer. In Zermatt, for example, the 12.5 per cent of visitors who choose not to ski can select from 38 mountain restaurants served by cable-car, chair-lift or funicular. The resort has 30 kilometres of footpaths, sleigh rides along the car-free streets, 15 indoor pools, a curling hall, ice rink, indoor golf, and language courses.

Counteracting seasonality

The trend towards non-skiers visiting ski resorts, would seem to support the premises that more all-round resorts – in which skiing is not the only activity – need to be developed, and that sporting and entertainment facilities need to be open throughout the year, rather than in just the winter months.

A key reason for ski destinations attracting limited investment is that skiing is perceived as a strictly seasonal business. Most ski resorts depend on winter activities to make or break their year. Few other industries exist solely from late autumn until spring. That is changing, albeit slowly. Many Alpine ski resorts have started to attract summer tourists by developing a wide range of sports and

Figure 7.3 Golf in Verbier – however, few resorts offer summer activities.

activities. Chair-lifts and cable-cars are operating for walking holidays – a growing summer activity. Many resorts already have swimming pools, skating rinks, tennis courts, guided walks, bike hire and, in some cases, glacier skiing. Others have started to advertise rock-climbing, white-river rafting, paragliding (parachuting off the mountainside), canyoning (abseiling down waterfalls), and hydrospeeding (swimming down white-water rapids on a specially designed surf board). However, more investment is required in many destinations, along with aggressive marketing policies to communicate the availability of these facilities.

The activities just enumerated are tempting the changing consumer – the active tourist who is no longer happy with sun, sand and sea. Resorts in the Austrian and French Alps are particularly well set up for such sports. Switzerland tends to cater more for walkers (Verbier, for example, has been very successful with its August music festivals). Tour operators to Italy focus almost exclusively on relaxing lake-side holidays with low-altitude walking. Unfortunately, many purpose-built ski resorts, especially in France, are not renowned for their aesthetic appeal. There are exceptions: Morzine and La Clusaz have managed to hang on to a measure of Alpine charm. In Austria, Alpbach and the Lech valley, and in Switzerland, Zermatt and Grindelwald, are among the most scenic. The diversification in activities does not only have a debatable cost, but also demands a great professionalism in order to offer very elaborate products. This diversification is, and will continue to be, facilitated by agreements between resorts.

The packaged multi-activity holiday is usually aimed at families, the biggest choice being in France. An increasing number of operators are starting to offer these summer holidays as an alternative to the Mediterranean. It is up to the Alpine destinations to ensure that they have the right product to cater for this growing market segment. However, although developing summer mountain tourism makes the most economic sense for resorts developed primarily for skiing (surplus accommodation already exists), the summer product is not as easily identified as the winter one. All winter resorts sell skiing, but few winter resorts offer summer activities (see Figure 7.3). Those resorts that take the lead in developing summer mountain tourism will be those that invest in research to understand the market, and that solve the problems of a complex product.

Market research

Many resorts are highly idiosyncratic in the way they collect and report information (Lewis and Wild 1995). In addition, some resorts and UK operators may inadvertently use wrong information in their marketing, and indeed some resorts may feel there are advantages to be gained through the continued use of some of the present inaccuracies. Yet in the long term this situation can only be harmful to all parties concerned.

In recent years there have been improvements in the way in which marketing messages have been compiled and communicated to customers, but although this information looks more 'glossy' and professional, the underlying marketing philosophy may not have been considered in any detail. There is a danger that resorts and operators are continuing to educate the market through promotional material to expect products that are sometimes impossible to deliver, and that are often quite costly in financial and environmental terms. The effectiveness of this marketing is becoming visible through some of the research being conducted on skiers' perceptions and destination choices (Hudson and Shephard 1998). In their article on service quality in ski resorts, Hudson and Shephard (1998) acknowledged that most customer satisfaction studies measure attributes that can make the product better, but never ask or deal with the actual *product* – the emotions. Managing this emotional experience requires the use of qualitative research tools such as focus groups and participant observation. Through understanding the emotional experience and by gaining very specific details on what needs to be altered, both the resort and the sport will be healthier.

Despite the financial investment and hard work that has gone into recent co-ordinated marketing efforts, there are still few examples of high-quality market research and analysis that can be used to compile and direct resort marketing communications. Much of resort advertising is designed specifically for the domestic market, and the majority is directed at sectors of the market already loyal to the destination. Marketing materials produced by resorts for the UK market are at best good translations of resort brochures. It is unlikely that such material will reach the right sectors of the UK market, or communicate the desired message that will attract more UK visitors to the Alps.

Conducting market research in the mountains (from the author's own experience) is not a straightforward task. As already discussed, on-site, intercept-and-quiz chair-lift surveys can be intrusive and problematic. The answer for European resorts may be the new point-of-view system (POV) used in Silver Mountain, Idaho (Newhart 1997). A customized survey composed of various types of questions is installed on a small metal box with a key-pad that allows guests to answer resort-specific questions privately at their own pace. The vendor periodically downloads the collected data via modem, eliminating time-consuming and expensive data entry. Updated results are available every two weeks, with a final comprehensive report issued at the end of each season.

Direct marketing

There is no reason why destinations in Europe cannot build relationships with customers and use direct mail to their advantage. At Killington, Vermont, the customer information database tracks 2.5 million skiers and grows by 200,000 skiers a year (Freedman 1992). The information – such as home address, level of skiing ability and past skiing expenditures – is culled from a variety of sources, including lodging facilities, rental shops, brochure requests and even random surveys of customers. The resort operator SKI Ltd also buys mailing lists from chambers of commerce and ski-related businesses. To gain the most out of its aggressive direct-mail and advertising efforts, SKI wields this information like a scalpel, dissecting its customer base to determine where its skiers come from, when they ski, what level they ski at, and what sorts of services they avail themselves of at the resort.

Destinations in Europe should consider following the example of their US counterparts, and invest in building a website on the Internet. The Swiss tourist office has taken a first step by launching a facility on its website that transmits live pictures from the ski slopes. Ski resorts can also take advantage of the direct-marketing opportunities that this new technology offers. One resort in the USA that has seen the traffic on its website increase dramatically is Sugerloaf, Maine. During the month of February, 1995, Sugerloaf distributed 49,958 pages of information about the resort, and this cost less than $800 (Carey 1995). The vehicle was a computer and modem with access to the Internet and world wide web.

Sugerloaf launched this project with a full-blown multimedia presentation that was unique in the industry. In the first ten days, 17,000 hits were recorded, and by March 1995 this number had risen to 55,000. The resort has found that skiers want up-to-date information on snow conditions and weather forecasts in a two-to-one margin over the next popular page, the piste map.

In Steamboat, Colorado, each of the 79 lodging properties at the resort has a page on the website that guests can peruse to plan their trips (Nelson 1997). To save paperwork and aid in making reservations, Steamboat developed a 'book-it' form that guests fill out and send via e-mail. One reservation clerk is assigned to handle the 60 to 80 contacts per day. She checks the inventory and e-mails a response. Guests then call in or fax the necessary credit card details, but Steamboat sees a time – relatively soon – when customers will trust e-mail with their credit card numbers.

A co-ordinated effort

More co-ordinated marketing is required, based on sound market research from European ski resorts. There have been recent examples of such efforts. In 1993 a strong publicity campaign was launched to attract visitors to the French Alps. This was the first time that a co-ordinated effort was made on such a scale, yet it revealed many of the old rivalries that exist between resorts (Lewis and Wild 1995). The title of the campaign was *La montagne ça vous gagne* (The mountain wins you over) and advertising was designed around the three themes of *amitié, environnement et diversité* (friendship, environment and diversity). This caused some of the larger resorts to look more closely at the information that they provide and to re-design and update advertising brochures. Two years later, Austria's top ski destinations joined together to boost business by forming their own marketing co-operative. The Top Ski Austria organization targeted the UK for its opening campaign, which was aimed across the board at experienced skiers, families and beginners.

Ski resorts in the Alps must somehow compete with the successful marketing skills of the North Americans, and it could take many years for countries like Switzerland to turn around the downturn in UK trade. The answer could be overall, co-ordinated marketing strategies that communicate a value-for-money message and cut through the bureaucracy and rivalry that exists among suppliers and resorts.

CONCLUSION

This chapter has focused on the future of the ski industry, a future that offers some exciting prospects. Despite the fact that the industry appears to have matured on both sides of the Atlantic, new changes in technology are generating some confidence in the future of winter sports. Skis that can make everyone a better skier, regardless of ability level, have profound operational and marketing implications.

There is still enormous potential, especially in Europe, for more sophisticated segmentation of markets by both destinations and operators. The non-skiing population has largely been ignored by marketers in the past, but is a segment that offers tremendous opportunity for growth. Similarly, more effort is required to understand and target growing market segments, such as the aging market, families and the long-haul market.

Bibliography

A. C. Nielsen (1998) *Holiday Booking Survey, 1997/98*, London: A. C. Nielsen.

Alexandris, K. and Carrol, B. (1997) 'Demographic differences in the perception of constraints on recreational sport participation: results from a study in Greece', *Leisure Studies*, 16(2), 107–25.

Arlidge, J. (1996) 'Scottish ski resorts hit by snow shortage', *Independent on Sunday*, 7 January.

Atchley, R. C. (1989) 'A continuity theory of normal aging', *Gerontologist*, 29, 183–90.

Balmer, D. (1995) 'Board trends may be the saviour of ski', *Travel Weekly*, 22 November, p. 7.

Barbier, B. (1978) 'Ski et stations de sports d'hiver dans le monde', *Weiner Geographische Schriften*, 52/52, 130–46.

Barbier, B. (1993) 'Problems of the French winter sports resorts', *Tourism Recreation Research*, 18(2), 5–11.

Barker, M. L. (1982) 'Traditional landscape and mass tourism in the Alps', *Geographical Review*, 72(4), 395–415.

Barker, M. L. (1994) 'Strategic tourism planning and limits to growth in the Alps', *Tourism Recreation Research*, 19(2),43–9.

Batchelor, D. E., Brewster, F., Carscallen, A. N., Douglas, H. P., Hall, F. A., McCorbey, A. A. and Mortureux, C. E. (1937) 'Skiing in Canada', *Canadian Geographical Journal*, 14(2), 57.

Beaudry, M. (1991) 'The limits to mountain resort growth', *Ski Area Management*, 30(3), 39–63.

Beeler, T. and Wood, J. (1990) 'Overcoming environmental obstacles', *Ski Area Management*, 29(2), 74–87.

Best, A. (1997) 'That's entertainment', *Ski Area Management*, 36(3), 66–89.

Boon, M. A. (1984) 'Understanding skiing behaviour', *Society and Leisure*, 7(2), 397–406.

Bosely, S. (1998) 'Medipack: injuries', *Guardian*, 7 November, Travel, p. 11.

Bray, R. (1995) 'Difficult market that could be on a slippery slope', *Travel Weekly*, 1 February.

Burkart, A. J. and Medlik, S. (1989) *Tourism: Past, Present, Future*, 2nd edn, London: Heinemann.

Burns, P. M. and Holden, A. (1995) *Tourism: A New Perspective*, London: Prentice Hall.

Carey, C. (1995) 'Loaf on the net', *Ski Area Management*, 34(3), 71.

Carmichael, B. (1992) 'Using conjoint modelling to measure tourist image and analyse ski resort choice', in Johnson, P. and Thomas, B. (eds) *Choice and Demand in Tourism*, pp. 93–106, London: Mansell.

Carmichael, B. (1996) 'Conjoint analysis of downhill skiers used to improve data collection for market segmentation', *Journal of Travel and Tourism Marketing*, 5(3), 187–206.

Castle, K. (1998) 'Skiing isn't just skiing anymore', *Ski Area Management*, 37(5), 47–8, 88.

Cater, E. and Lowman, G. (eds) (1994) *Ecotourism: A Sustainable Option?*, New York: John Wiley & Sons.

Chadwick, R. A. (1987) 'Concepts, definitions and measures used in travel and tourism research', in Ritchie, J. R. B. and Goeldner, C. R. (eds) *Travel, Tourism and Hospitality Research*, pp. 47–61, New York: Wiley.

Chissel, H. R., Feagin Jr, J. A., Warme, W. J., Lambert, K. L., King, P. and Johnson, L. (1996) 'Trends in ski and snowboard injuries', *Sports Medicine*, 22(3), 141–5.

Cleverdon, R. and Edwards, E. (1982) *International Tourism to 1990*, Cambridge: Abt Books.

Cockerell, N. (1988) 'Skiing in Europe – potential and problems', *EIU Travel and Tourism Analyst*, 5, 66–81.

Cockerell, N. (1994) 'Market segments: the international ski market in Europe', *EIU Travel and Tourism Analyst*, 3, 34–55.

Colorado Board of Tourism (1992) *Colorado Consumer Study*, Denver: CBT.

Cooper, C. P. (ed.) (1989) *Progress in Tourism, Recreation and Hospitality Management*, vol. 3, London: Belhaven.

Cooper, C., Fletcher, J., Gilbert, D. and Wanhill, S. (1993) *Tourism: Principles and Practice*, London: Pitman Publishing.

Crystal Holidays (1996) 'The ski industry report'.

Crystal Holidays (1997) 'The 96/97 ski industry report'.

Csikszentmihalyi, M. (1975) *Beyond Boredom and Anxiety*, San Francisco: Jossey-Bass Publishers.

Dilley, R. S. and Pozihun, P. (1986) 'Skiers in Thunder Bay, Ontario: perceptions and behaviour', *Recreation Research Review*, 12(4), 27–32.

East, M. (1998) 'Manias for takeovers ready to infect the High Street', *Travel Weekly*, 14 October, p. 6.

Edgell, D. L.(1990) *International Tourism Policy*, New York: Van Nostrand Reinhold.

English, N. (1996) 'A Swiss love affair that's rapidly heading downhill', *Mail on Sunday*, 28 January.

Ewing, G. O. and Kulka, T. (1979) 'Revealed and stated preference analysis of ski resort attractiveness', *Leisure Sciences*, 2 (3/4), 249–75.

Faison, E. W. (1961) 'Effectiveness of one-sided and two-sided mass communications in advertising', *Public Opinion Quarterly*, 16, 248–55.

Fernald, R. (1986) 'Matching the market mix', *Ski Area Management*, 25(5), 44–6.

Foxhall, G. R. and Goldsmith, R. E. (1994) *Consumer Psychology for Marketing*, London: Routledge.

Fraser, I. (1990) 'Out of the slush and into the bunker', *Eurobusiness*, December, 28–31.

Freedman, D. H. (1992) 'An unusual way to run a ski business', *Forbes*, 7(12), 27–32.

Fry, J. (1995) 'Exactly what are their environmental attitudes?', *Ski Area Management*, 34(4), 45–70.

Gilbert, D. C.(1990) 'Conceptual issues in the meaning of tourism', in Cooper, C. (ed.) *Progress in Tourism, Recreation and Hospitality Management*, vol. 2, part 1, pp. 78–105, London: Belhaven.

Gillen, B. and Best, S. (1991) 'How the Brits see us', *Ski Area Management*, 30(4), 41–64.

Glyptis, S. A. (1991) 'Sport and tourism', in Cooper, C. P. (ed.) *Progress in Tourism, Recreation and Hospitality Management*, vol. 3, pp. 165–83, London: Belhaven.

Goeldner, C. R. (1978) 'The Colorado skier: 1977–78 season', Business Research Division, Graduate School of Business, University of Colorado.

Goeldner, C. R. (1996) '1994–1995 economic analysis', *Ski Area Management*, 35(3), 76.

Goeldner, C. R. and Standley, S. (1980) 'Skiing trends', in *Proceedings: 1980 National Outdoor Recreation Trends Symposium*, Durham, New Hampshire, US. Department of Agriculture, vol. 1, pp. 105–20.

Goodall, B. and Bergsma, J. R. (1993) 'Tour operators' strategies: a cross-country comparison', in Sinclair, M. T. and Stabler, M. J. (eds) *The Tourism Industry: An International Analysis*, pp. 91–106, Wallingford, Oxon: CAB International.

Grabowski, P. (1992) 'White gold', *In Focus*, 5, 8–9.

Greer, S. (1990) 'Snow business', *Leisure Management*, 10(2), 34–5.

Hager, B. (1989) 'Wall Street perspective', *Ski Area Management*, 28(3), 86–91.

Haid, H. (1989) *Vom Neuen Leben. Alternative Wirtschaftsund Lebensformen in den Alpen*, Innsbruck: Hayman.

Harbaugh, J. A. (1997) 'Ski industry consolidation or financing 90s Style?', *Ski Area Management*, 36(4), 51–2, 74.

Hardy, P. (1994) 'Star-spangled service', *Daily Telegraph*, 5 November.

Hardy, P. (1997) 'Boards are big – carving will be bigger', *Daily Telegraph*, 22 February.

Hawkins, D. E. (1994) 'Ecotourism: opportunities for developing countries', in Theobald, W. (ed.) *Global tourism*, Oxford: Butterworth Heinemann.

Heard, D. (1995) 'Skiing', *Travel Weekly*, 31 May, 37–40.

Heard, D. (1996) 'Ski preview', *Travel Weekly*, 29 May, 37–40.

Heineman, K. (1986) 'The future of sports: challenge for the science of sport', *International Review for the Sociology of Sport*, 24(4).

Henderson, K. A., Stalnaker, D. and Taylor, G. (1988) 'The relationship between barriers to recreation and gender-role personality traits for women', *Journal of Leisure Research*, 20(2), 69–80.

Herzog, L. (1996) 'Whistler resort', *Hotelier*, January–February, 31–3.

Hodgson, A. (ed.) (1987) *The Travel and Tourism Industry*, Oxford: Pergamon.

Holden, A. (1998) 'The use of visitor understanding in skiing management and development decisions at the Cairngorm Mountains, Scotland', *Tourism Management*, 19(2), 145–52.

Holloway, J. C. (1990) *The Business of Tourism*, Plymouth: MacDonald and Evans.

Holloway, J. C. and Plant, R. V. (1988) *Marketing for Tourism: A Practical Guide*, Harlow: Longman.

Hovland, C. I., Janis, I. L. and Kelley, H. H. (1948) *Experiments on Mass Communication*, Princeton, NJ: Princeton University Press.

Hudson, S. (1995) 'Responsible tourism: a model for the greening of Alpine ski resorts', in Fleming, S., Talbot, M. and Tomlinson, A. (eds) *Policy and Politics in Sport, Education and Leisure*, pp. 239–55, Brighton: LSA Publications.

Hudson, S. (1996) 'The "greening" of ski resorts: a necessity for sustainable tourism, or a marketing opportunity for skiing communities?', *Journal of Vacation Marketing*, 2(2), 176–85.

Hudson, S. (1998a) 'Tourism constraints: an empirical test of the hierarchical model of constraints', in Hsu C. H. C. (ed.) *Proceedings of the New Frontiers in Tourism Research Conference*, pp. 165–80, Cleveland, OH.

Hudson, S. (1998b) 'There's no business like snow business! Marketing skiing into the 21st century', *Journal of Vacation Marketing*, 4(4), 393–407.

Hudson, S. (1998c) 'An extension of leisure constraints theory related to the consumer behaviour of skiing', Unpublished PhD thesis, University of Surrey, Guildford.

Hudson, S. and Shephard, G. W. (1998) 'Measuring service quality at tourist destinations: an application of importance–performance analysis to an Alpine ski resort', *Journal of Travel and Tourism Marketing*, 7(3), 61–77.

Hunt, J. D. and Layne, D. (1992) 'Evolution of travel and tourism terminology and definitions', *Journal of Travel Research*, 29(4), 7–11.

Isham, J. (1996) 'Zone therapy for beginners', *Ski Area Management*, 35(2), 68–9.

Jackson, E. L. (1993) 'Recognising patterns of leisure constraints: results from alternative analysis', *Journal of Leisure Research*, 25(2), 129–49.

Jackson, E. L. and Dunn, E. (1988) 'Integrating ceasing participation with other aspects of leisure behaviour', *Journal of Leisure Research*, 20(1), 31–45.

Jackson, E. L. and Henderson, K. (1995) 'Gender-based analysis of leisure constraints', *Leisure Sciences*, 17(1), 31–51.

Jafari, J. (1977) 'Editor's page', *Annals of Tourism Research*, 6(11), 6–11.

Jones, S. (1998) 'Early lunch aims to haul back market share', *Travel Weekly*, 18 March.

Kay, T. and Jackson, G. (1991) 'Leisure despite constraint: the impact of leisure constraints on leisure participation', *Journal of Leisure Research*, 23(4), 301–13.

Keating, M. (1991) 'Bad sports', *Geographical*, 63, 26–9.

Keogh, B. (1980) 'Motivations and the choice decision of skiers', *Tourist Review*, 35(1), 18–22.

Kiernan, P. (1992) 'Earth-bound', *Marketing Week*, August 21, 26–30.

Klenosky, D. B., Gengler, C. E. and Mulvey, M. S. (1993) 'Understanding the factors influencing ski destination choice: a means-end analytical approach', *Journal of Leisure Research*, 25(4), 326–79.

Kotler, P. (1982) *Principles of Marketing*, 2nd edn, Englewood Cliffs, NJ: Prentice Hall.

Kottke, M. (1990) 'Growth trends: going both ways at once', *Ski Area Management*, 29(1), 63–4, 96–7.

Krippendorf, J. (1986) *Alpsegen – Alptraum. Für eine Tourismus-Entwicklung im Einklang mit Mensch und Natur*, Bern, Switzerland: Kümmerly & Frey.

Krippendorf, J. (1987) *The Holidaymakers*, London: Heinemann.

Krippendorf, J., Zommer, P. and Glauber, H. (eds) (1988) *Von der Diskrepanz zwischen Zielen und*

Wirklichkeit. In Für Einen Andern Tourismus, Frankfurt: Fischer Verlang.

Lane, B. (1992) 'Marketing green tourism', *Leisure Opportunities*, January, 34–5.

Lazard, A. J. (1996) 'Gathering stats worldwide', *Ski Area Management*, 35(5), 60–73.

Leiweke, T. (1996) 'Leading the charge: can we grow the sport? Absolutely!' *Ski Area Management*, 35(2), 16–18.

Lewis, R. and Wild, M. (1995) 'French ski resorts and UK ski tour operators', The Centre for Tourism Occasional Papers, Sheffield Hallam University.

Lewis, S. (1997) 'Ski update', *Travel Weekly*, 16 April, 69.

Lewis, S. and Bird, L. (1997) 'Ski update', *Travel Weekly*, 7 May, 53–5.

Liebers, A. (1963) *The Complete Book of Winter Sports*, New York: Coward-McCann.

Lundberg, D. E. (1989) *The Tourism Business*, 6th edn, New York: Van Nostrand Reinhold.

Martinelli, M. (1976) 'Meteorology and ski area development and operation', in *Proceedings: Fourth National Conference on Fire and Forest Meteorology*, USDA, RM–52.

Mathieson, A. and Wall, G. (1982) *Tourism: Economic, Physical and Social Impacts*, Harlow: Longman.

Maurer, J. (1996) 'Ethnic marketing', *Ski Area Management*, 35(3), 59–60.

May, V. (1995) 'Environmental implications of the 1992 Winter Olympic Games', *Tourism Management*, 16(4), 269–75.

McIntosh, R. W. and Goeldner, C. R. (1986) *Tourism Principles, Practices, Philosophies*, New York: John Wiley.

McKinsey & Company (1989) *Ski Area Management*, 28(2), 65.

Messerli, P. (1987) 'The development of tourism in the Swiss Alps: economic, social, and environmental effects. Experiences and recommendations from the Swiss MAB Programme', *Mountain Research and Development*, 7, 13–24.

Middleton, V. T. C. (1988) *Marketing in Travel and Tourism*, London: Heinemann.

Mills, A. S. (1985) 'Participation motivations for outdoor recreation: a test of Maslow's theory', *Journal of Leisure Research*, 17(3), 184–99.

Mills, A. S., Couturier, H. and Snepenger, D. J. (1986) 'Segmenting Texas snow skiers', *Journal of Travel Research*, 25(2), 19–23.

Mintel (1994) 'Skiing', *Leisure Intelligence*, vol. 2, pp. 1–24, London: Mintel International Group Ltd.

Mintel (1996) *Snowsports*, June, pp. 1–35, London: Mintel International Group Ltd.

National Ski Areas Association (1994) 'Enhance ski areas' environmental image', *Ski Area Management*, 33(1).

Nelson, J. (1995a) 'How Disney does it', *Ski Area Management*, 34(4), 41.

Nelson, J. (1995b) 'Turning trails into classrooms', *Ski Area Management*, 34(6), 48.

Nelson, J. (1996) 'Maybe the message is flow', *Ski Area Management*, 35(3), 13.

Nelson, J. (1997) 'A salesman in cyberspace', *Ski Area Management*, 36(3), 70–1.

Newhart, T. (1997) 'Suggestion box goes high-tech', *Ski Area Management*, 36(3), 50.

Newsom, S. (1996) 'Single minded', *Sunday Times*, 8 December, pp. 6–7.

O'Callaghan, J. (1996) 'Winter escape', *Conference and Incentive Travel*, November–December, 93–6.

Olcott, D. (1996) 'Learning parks', *Ski Area Management*, 35(2), 54.

Otten, L. and King, S. (1996) '"STEEP" analysis of industry', *Ski Area Management*, 35(2), 12–13.

Packer, J. (1998) 'Everything you ever wanted to know about ski and snowboard tourists but were afraid to ask', *Journal of Vacation Marketing*, 4(2), 186–92.

Pearce, D. G. (1978) 'Tourist development: two processes', *Travel Research Journal*, 43–51.

Pearce, D. G. (1987) *Tourism Today: A Geographical Analysis*, Harlow: Longman.

Pearce, D. G. (1995) *Tourism Development*, Harlow: Longman.

Perla, R. and Glenn, B. (1981) 'Skiing', in Gray, D. M. and Male, D. H. (eds) *Handbook of Snow: Principles, Processes, Management and Use*, Pergamon: Toronto.

Petrick, T. (1996) 'Significant growth', *Ski Area Management*, 35(2), 65.

'Portrait of a skiing enthusiast', *Precision Marketing*, 15 February 1993, p. 8.

Preau, P. (1968) 'Essai d'une typologie de stations de sports d'hiver dans les Alpes du Nord', *Revue de Geographie Alpine*, 58(1), 127–40.

Preau, P. (1970) 'Principe d'analyse des sites en montagne', *Urbanisme*, 116, 21–5.

Rand, A. (1995) 'Marketing to ski clubs', *Ski Area Management*, 34(4), 44–62.

Rand, A. (1996) 'What do teenagers want?', *Ski Area Management*, 35(3), 61–3.

Raymore, L., Godbey, G., Crawford, D. and von Eye, A. (1993) 'Nature and process of leisure constraints: an empirical test', *Leisure Sciences*, 15(2), 99–113.

Raymore, L. A., Godbey, G. C. and Crawford, D. W. (1994) 'Self-esteem, gender, and socioeconomic status: their relation to perception of constraints on leisure among adolescents', *Journal of Leisure Research*, 26(2), 99–118.

Richards, G. (1995) 'Retailing travel products: bridging the information gap', *Progress in Tourism and Hospitality Research*, 1(1), 17–29.

Robinson, H. (1976) *A Geography of Tourism*, London: MacDonald & Evans.

Rosall, N. (1998) 'Internet's explosive growth – an overview', *Ski Area Management*, 28(2), 51–3, 76.

Rowan, D. (1989) 'Lifts 1988', *Ski Area Management*, 28(2), 74–6.

Rowan, J. (1997) 'Bringing snowmaking to the public', *Ski Area Management*, 36(2), 49.

Ryan, C. (1991) 'Tourism and marketing – a symbiotic relationship?', *Tourism Management*, 12, 101–11.

Sadruddin, Prince, the Aga Khan (1994) 'Tourism and a European strategy for the Alpine environment', in Cater, E. and Lowman, G. (eds) *Ecotourism: A sustainable option*, pp. 103–10, New York: John Wiley & Sons.

Sager, D. (1996) 'Future perfect', *Ski Survey*, February–March, 6–7.

Scharff, R. (ed.) (1974) *Ski Magazine's Encyclopaedia of Skiing*, New York: Universal.

Scott, A. (1994) 'We have lift-off', *Sunday Times*, 3 June.

Scott, A. (1995) 'Gearing up', *Sunday Times*, 19 November.

Scott, A. (1998) 'It's simply the biggest – and simply the best', *Sunday Times*, 27 September.

Scott, D. and Jackson, E. L. (1996) 'Factors that limit and strategies that might encourage people's use of public parks', *Journal of Park and Recreation Administration*, 14(1), 1–17.

Shaw, S. M., Bonen, A. and McCabe, J. F. (1991) 'Do more constraints mean less leisure? Examining the relationship between constraints and participation', *Journal of Leisure Research*, 23(4), 286–300.

Sibley, R. G. (1982) 'Ski resort planning and development', Foundation for the Technical Advancement of Local Government Engineering in Victoria, Melbourne.

Simon, B. (1996) 'Building security against no-snow days', *Financial Times*, 14 February.

Sinclair, M. T. and Stabler, M. J. (1993) 'New perspectives on the tourism industry', in Sinclair, M. T. and Stabler, M. J. (eds) *The Tourism Industry: An International Analysis*, pp. 1–14, Wallingford, Oxon: CAB International.

'Ski Preview', *Travel Weekly*, 1996, pp. 37–40.

Skidmore, J. (1998) 'Thomson beats rivals to £66m Crystal purchase', *Travel Weekly*, 26 August, p. 1.

Smith, S. L. J. (1983) *Recreation Geography*, London: Longman.

Sports Council (1991) *A Digest of Sport Statistics for the UK*, London: Sports Council.

Spring, J. (1995a) 'Age-group marketing', *Ski Area Management*, 34(3), 60.

Spring, J. (1995b) 'Are we on the brink of a boom?', *Ski Area Management*, 34(4), 39–68.

Spring, J. (1996a) 'More days/more fun but shrinking numbers', *Ski Area Management*, 35(4), 44–5.

Spring, J. (1996b) 'European skiers: not so different', *Ski Area Management*, 35(5), 61–80.

Spring, J. (1997) 'Crossovers fuel boarding', *Ski Area Management*, 36(3), 55–6.

Spring, J. (1998) 'Subtle but important shifts in customers', *Ski Area Management*, 37(5), 57–8.

Stewart, F. (1993) 'UK leisure trends and the prospects after skiing', paper presented at 1993 National Ski Conference, Olympia, London.

Stokes, D. (1996) 'Work in', *Hotelier*, January–February, 23–9.

Swarbrooke, J. (1994) 'Greening and competitive advantage', *Insights*, May, D 43–50.

Tanler, B. (1966) 'A decade of growth', *Ski Area Management*, 5(4), 10–14.

Taylor, S. (1997) 'Ski Club of Great Britain: business growth plan 1998–2003', prepared by Ski Club of Great Britain, London.

'The US adventure travel industry', *Travel Trade Gazette*, 7 May 1997, p. 83.

Theobald, W. F. (1994) 'The context, meaning and scope of tourism', in Theobald, W. F. (ed.), *Global Tourism*, pp. 3–19, Oxford: Butterworth-Heinemann Ltd.

Tikalsky, F. T. and Lahren, S. L. (1988) 'Why people ski', *Ski Area Management*, 27(3), 68–114.

Todd, S. E. and Williams, P. W. (1996) 'From white to green: a proposed environmental management system framework for ski areas', *Journal of Sustainable Tourism*, 4(3), 147–73.

Travel Industry Association of America (1992) *Tourism and the Environment*, Washington, DC: Travel Industry Association of America.

United States Bureau of the Census (1979) *National Travel Survey: Travel During 1977*, Washington, DC: US Government Printing Office.

Urry, J. (1990) *The Tourist Gaze: Leisure and Travel in Contemporary Societies*, London: Sage.

Uysal, M., Howard, G. and Jamrozy, U. (1991) 'An application of importance–performance analysis to a ski resort: a case study in North Carolina', *Visions in Leisure and Business*, 10(1), 16–25.

'Virgin's high-tech "brochure" triumph' (1996) *Journal of Travel Marketing*, November, p. 38.

Wickers, D. (1994) 'Snow alternative', *Sunday Times*, 27 November, p. 9.

Wight, P. (1994) 'Environmentally responsible marketing of tourism', in Cater, E. and Lowman, G. (eds) *Ecotourism: A Sustainable Option*, pp. 39–55. New York: John Wiley & Son.

Williams, P. (1993) 'The evolution of the skiing industry', in Khan, M. A., Olsen, M. D. and van Var, T. (eds) *VNR's Encyclopaedia of Hospitality and Tourism*, pp. 926–33, New York: Nostrand Reinhold.

Williams, P. W. and Basford, R. (1992) 'Segmenting downhill skiing's latent demand markets', *American Behavioural Scientist*, 36(2), 222–35.

Williams, P. and Dossa, K. (1990) *British Columbia Downhill Skier Survey 1989–90. B.C. Ministry of Tourism*. The Centre for Tourism Policy and Research, Simon Fraser University, and Canada West Ski Areas Association.

Williams, P. W. and Dossa, K. B. (1995) 'Canada's ski markets', *Ski Area Management*, 34(5), 62–3.

Williams, P. W. and Dossa, K. B. (1998) 'Ski channel users: a discriminating perspective', *Journal of Travel and Tourism Marketing*, 7(2), 1–29.

Williams, P. W., Dossa, K. B. and Fulton, A. (1994) 'Tension on the slopes: managing conflict between skiers and snowboarders', *Journal of Applied Recreation Research*, 19(3), 191–213.

Williams, P. W. and Hayden, S. (1986) *Ski Tracks to the Future: Key Dimensions of Beginner and Non-skier Markets*, Toronto: Canadian Ski Council and Fitness Canada.

Williams, P. W. and Lattey, C. (1994) 'Skiing constraints for women', *Journal of Travel Research*, 33(2), 21–5.

Wilson, A. (1996) 'Where the wild things are', *Sunday Times*, 20 October, p. 15.

'Winter Wonderlands', *The Economist*, 31 January 1998, p. 86.

Witchel, D. B. (1989) 'The Seniors Are Coming', *Ski Area Management*, 28(4), 54–78.

Witchel, D. B. (1996) 'What Do Mothers Want?', *Ski Area Management*, 35(1), 64–89.

Witt, S. F. and Moutinho, L. (eds) (1994) *Tourism Marketing Management Handbook*, 2nd edn, Hemel Hempstead: Prentice-Hall International.

Wood, K. (1992) *The Good Tourist. A Worldwide Guide for the Green Traveller*, London: Mandarin.

World Tourism Organization (WTO) (1992) 'Tourism Trends to the Year 2000 and Beyond', research report presented by Robert Cleverdon at EXPO Seville, September 1992.

World Tourism Organization (1998) 'Leading the world's largest industry', http:www.//worldtourism-org.

World Travel and Tourism Council (1995) 'Travel and tourism's economic perspective', special report, January.

Wright, B. A. and Goodale, T. L. (1991) 'Beyond non-participation: validation of interest and frequency of participation categories in constraints research', *Journal of Leisure Research*, 23(4), 314–31.

Zimmer, Z., Brayley, R. E. and Searle, M. (1995) 'Whether to go and where to go: identification of important influences on seniors' decisions to travel', *Journal of Travel Research*, 33(3), 3–10.

Index